KERB — 26

Journal of
Landscape
Architecture

2018

••

Kerb is published annually by:
Uro Publications, Melbourne, Australia
uropublications.com.

ISBN 9780648435549
ISSN 1324-8049

Printed in Singapore.
Distributed in Australia by Books at Manic and internationally by Idea Books.

Each edition of **Kerb** is produced by a new student editorial team.

••

Kerb 26 editorial team
Albert Rex
Jesika Ellul
Julie Demary
Michelle Thomas Zacaharias
Rachel Floch
Will Muhleisen

Supervising editors
Charles Anderson - **Kerb** 26 Supervisor
Bridget Keane
Heike Rahmann

Production consultants
Karina Smith - Copy Editor

••

Art direction
Sean Hogan – Trampoline.
trampoline.net.au

Graphic design
A collaboration between the editorial team and Sean Hogan - Trampoline.

Acknowledgments
The editorial team would like to thank everyone involved in the production of the journal for their heartening generosity, enthusiasm and patience in what drew out into quite a lengthy editorial process.

••

Front cover imagery
The One Who Checks & The One Who Balances
2018 – ongoing.
Futuristic regalia by artist Cannupa Hanska Luger with beadwork by artist Kathy Whitman-Elk Woman
Photo still, regalia for performance series
Beadwork, surplus industrial felt, ceramic, riot gear, afghan.

Title page/ Section dividers / Contributors page / Contents page photography
Louis Mitchell

THIS PUBLICATION CONTAINS IMAGES
OF PEOPLE WHO HAVE DIED

Landscape
Architecture

TWO UP
FRIDAYS
9PM

ENGAGING RESILIENTLY

ENGAGING CRITICALLY

ENGAGING COLLABORATIVELY

Editorial

Albert Rex
Jesika Ellul
Julie Demary
Michelle Thomas Zacharias
Rachel Floch
Will Muhleisen

Over the last 600 years, European colonial expansion and resource extraction has reshaped the globe. It has displaced and marginalised myriad peoples, relationships and lands across the planet and resulted in the deep hurt and fracture we now witness across our contemporary 'global community'.

Landscape architecture, which we define as a Western school of thought born of the English Romantic movement, is a discipline produced by, and so complicit in, these power structures.

Moreover, landscape architects today operate with a degree of influence over the authorship of space. Should landscape architects wish to, they could assist in erasing proud histories with an idle stroke on a page. So too, by engaging in careful collaboration, they could begin to work in new ways with traditional custodians and other groups that Western societies have tended in the past to at best ignore and at worst suppress.

With this in mind, the editors of Kerb 26 walked toward each other on the theme "Homelands", defined in our eyes as aiming to shine a light on the global conditions and prospects of fragmented, displaced and marginalised peoples as well as the complex realities of often asymmetric, cross-cultural exchange.

Is landscape architecture not a discipline that prides itself on an embrace of multiplicity? Ian McHarg's work in ecology teaches us that a complex system is a healthy and resilient one, Giles Clement's 'Third Landscape' embraces not the freedom of growth, but specifically the celebration of small, fragile and niche ecologies, and the German industrial parks movement positions the discipline clearly as having the capacity to not just embrace history, but support destabilised life-worlds as they consolidate and expand their role into the twenty-first century.

Of course, we are not suggesting that landscape architects and designers do, or should, hold any kind of monopoly over the production of space. Indeed, a large body of work presented in this journal is of a vernacular nature; produced by individuals and small groups specifically because the larger European-derived design traditions have failed to cater to their needs and practices. While our journal prioritises the accounts of homelands that have been threatened, attacked or subsumed, we hope the reader will bear in mind the broader readings of the theme, wherein we all have a homeland.

We hope that in acknowledging the importance of homelands as essential to everyone, we introduce a common element to an otherwise disparate theme: the earth. The earth as home raises notions of responsibility, not only toward a delimited area prescribed as 'home', but toward our planet as a whole.

There are some within the design fields who already embrace one or more of these readings of homelands, and in doing so are already counteracting deeply ingrained standards and norms in their respective disciplines. Vernacular or "ethno-architects" are at the same time working on the production of their own spaces, this generates a climate with unprecedented opportunity for the expression of thoroughly varied "homelands". And so Kerb 26 highlights and celebrates the work of the many among us already taking steps in this direction, as well as providing examples, inspiration and confidence for others who hope to do so in the future.

The journal has been divided into three broad categories, all of which centre on the idea of engaging with the issue of homelands in different ways. Based on our observations, some practitioners engage resiliently while others engage critically and yet more engage collaboratively.

Obviously, there is a clear overlap and interface between these categories. We definitely appreciate the irony of broadly categorising a journal that is meant to celebrate work that sits in defiance of standard categorisations. However, we believe that framing the work in terms of how different practitioners engage with the issue helps to provide readers with clear actionable ways of engaging with the theme.

ENGAGING RESILIENTLY

Many contributors have shone a light on resilient designs and practices. These involve work that has safeguarded cultural practices through design thinking. Gautham Sarang celebrates the vernacular community-sourced architecture of Kerala. Not always tidy and rarely economically sensible, these works are nonetheless an embodiment of a long-developed sense of place. In even starker response to the colonial settler, Émelie Desrochers-Turgeon celebrates the nomadicity of adaptive architecture in Nunavut. By appropriating colonial buildings, local people have developed mobile structures that allow for the transport of goods between communities, and so fought back against the imposition of a sedentary lifestyle.

ENGAGING CRITICALLY

Other contributors have taken a more critical approach to the theme. These include essays, design propositions and analyses that aim to interrogate and question contemporary modes of practice and the effects that these have on Indigenous and other minority groups. Maria Trovato documents the exhausting spatial hardships imposed on both refugees and their hosts after crossing into temporary homelands. Julia Watson critiques the societal ignorance of Indigenous innovations. And Pierre Bélanger unpacks the entangled history of Canada's national parks with the forced resettlement of Indigenous peoples. By engaging with contemporary Western discourse on its own terms, these practitioners do a lot to hold the inadequacies and problems of our societies to account.

ENGAGING COLLABORATIVELY

Another group of contributors are those who we see as engaging collaboratively. These are practitioners who walk the line of what Sophia Pearce and Jock Gilbert call the "cultural interface". Jefa Greenaway and Indigenous Architecture and Design Victoria's engagement with the University of Melbourne and Australia's broader architectural community is a fantastic example of this more pragmatic approach. These practitioners look not only at supporting the oppressed or questioning the oppressor, but produce work that hopes to build and strengthen ties between these traditionally oppositional parties.

In sum, Kerb 26 is about engagement with "homelands". In celebrating the work of a wide range of practitioners already engaged with the issue, we hope our journal provides a pathway for others to do the same in an informed, invigorated and respectful way.

ENGAGING

RESILIENTLY

HOMES THAT WEAVE PEOPLE TOGETHER

Gautham Sarang

There is a sure correspondence between the architecture of a place and the character of the community that has settled there. Architecture plays a key role in whether a community crumbles or comes together.

Marwa Al-Sabouni,
Architect and author of The Battle for Home,
2016.

Attappady, my homeland, is a hilly region on the Western Ghats of India. Unlike villages in the other parts of the country where the houses are concentrated in one place, families and households are scattered throughout the area with their own farmlands on the hilltops and valleys. We have people from various cultures in this region. Some migrated here centuries ago, some decades ago. Once upon a time, activities like running to the river half a kilometre down a sixty degree slope were an everyday fun thing for kids and elders alike. However, after the roads started creeping into our land, our village became "remote" and things like climbing the hills became a "hardship". My homeland was encroached upon by "development". This is my story of building a "home" in my homeland.

We moved to the village thirty-five years ago. My first friend in the village was Jooli, a boy little older than me. His language was Irula and mine, Malayalam. Naturally, we learnt both the languages. So did most of the kids in our region. There used to be unique patterns in everything cultural including architecture. From low grass thatched roofs to tiled roofs marked with completion dates on the sides. We had a healthy diversity in architecture. There was also quite a bit of exchange of knowledge and practices among these cultures. Communities learned and were inspired by each other. There were no appointed architects, and like all the other beings on the planet, people knew how to build homes with locally available materials. Over the years each community developed an architectural vocabulary according to their environment.

My parents built our house with adobe bricks. Jooli's parents were into wattle and daub. Both of the families had grass thatched roofs. My father was proud of his comparatively thin roof that used less grass. Jooli's father was into thick roofs with a different variety of grasses. Both our houses had cow dung plastered over a beaten mud floor. Jooli's mother polished the floor with round stones she got from the river. Even their walls were polished over the seasons. My mother also learned this technique from Jooli's mother and other ladies in the village. Hence, our floor also started looking fancy! Mathai and Ammini, our other neighbours, baked adobe bricks in their impromptu kiln even though they still used mud for mortar. Vidyasagar's house was about a kilometre away from our homes. His father was a carpenter and thus, a "recognised architect" of his times. Apart from the baked bricks and mud mortar, they had symmetrical wooden doors and windows. Many in our village had doors made of bamboo. Door locks were not common in our village and apart from a chain or a rope that held the door to the frame, there were no fancy fittings on them.

As you can see, I grew up immersed in vernacular architecture, just like all the other kids in my village. Most of the construction was done by family

Cashew oil being used to preserve timber members.

members. Experts and additional hands were hired as and when needed. Most of the masonry work was done by masons while adobe brick making was a family affair. We kids had fun mixing the mud for adobe bricks or for mortar. If the bricks were to be baked, things were done under an expert's supervision. Grass thatching was again done by the family and so was the floor. Men, women and children had their own roles to play through the entire construction process.

Every new construction or piece of maintenance taught us kids something or the other. We all learned about the trees that can be used for columns, roof or wattle. We learned the kind of soil that can be used for bricks, floors or ovens. We experimented with ratios in mud mortar, slope for the roof and thickness in grass thatching. While the construction was on, our parents didn't spend a lot of time parenting. However, we always used to go around with them and watch their work with wonder. We also loved trying to catch up with the techniques. None of our parents were architects or building contractors, yet they knew how to build a complete structure from scratch with the locally available materials.

Building homes brought the community together. Working together was a way of socialising. People ate together, sitting around on the heaps of mud or dried adobe bricks during this development. Working in the sun and being in the mud was the most natural thing for everyone. Our "tech-lore" was open source and all the materials were local. The people involved knew their roles and what they were doing. I learned technical terms like adobe, mud architecture, wattle and daub, mud plastering, etc. They have been household subjects for a very long time. There were innovations, exchanges and experiments in all these. I remember government providing financial support to certain communities for maintenance of mud houses and also promoting such sustainable technology. Irrespective of their social standing, every community was empowered with their respective tech-lore.

Earlier, the land had a role to play in people's lives. People had a role to play in making a land their homeland. Everyone was dependent upon natural resources. Attappady provided for all the communities with clean air, water, fertile soil, material for construction, fuel wood, medicines and livelihoods of various sorts. Unwittingly we were rooted in our homeland with all the provisions it had. Everyone was productively occupied. Friendship grew beyond communities through social activities like fishing, agriculture, festivals and such. People respected the authenticity of their homeland. But not anymore.

External influences gradually affected priorities. Livelihood statuses and needs changed. One did not have to grow his own food anymore. Communities started getting tagged as "primitive" and "modern". Timber and bamboo no longer qualified as construction materials. Curries with seasonal bamboo shoot, cherry tomatoes, fresh river fish, abundant papaya or pumpkins fell into the primitive category. Growing millets went out of fashion. Cabbage, carrots and big shiny tomatoes bought from the market became the modern statement while any traditional livelihood practices fell into the primitive category. Communities that depended on the market solely for trading their cattle and getting their necessities became mere consumers. In the name of development, government and non-governmental agencies poured money into self-respecting communities. Alcoholism and consumerism seeped into the remotest of the villages. The connection one had to the homeland was severed. The strong but flexible, wattle-like inter- and intra-community bonds started cracking.

Indigenous people tried to become Malayalis. They avoided talking in their dialect in front of other communities. Malayali and Tamil people got busy teaching their kids English. Communities convinced their young that their homeland was primitive and pushed them toward opportunities outside Attappady so that they could escape from the "hardships" of their homeland. For many youngsters now, their homeland is an alien land, which they are embarrassed to acknowledge.

Jooli is building his new house. He got a grant from the government. The grant comes in instalments and requires him to conform to modern building techniques like a concrete roof. Unlike old times, now Jooli can only do some of the work like digging for the foundation or mixing concrete. Everything else has to be done by an expert or semi-expert mason. At each stage (foundation, walls, roof, wiring and plumbing), the work is evaluated by officials. If the progress does not please them, then the next instalment is delayed. Material prices go up with every passing day, forcing Jooli to borrow money. He has less time for his daughter since he has to go logging, which pays him well. It is very common in Attappady to sell trees and culms of bamboo for money. Homeland is not seen as a provider anymore. It is a huge market where you sell anything possible to get the modern version of cloth, food and shelter.

How did this happen? Was it the modern education, awareness of the mainstream, globalisation, the government policies? Or was it the agenda of the contractor-politician official nexus? Maybe a little of all of these. As a result, even the diversity of architecture is almost dead in Attappady. Everyone owns, or wishes to build, only concrete houses in various sizes shapes and colours. Everything is done by machines, experts and contractors. Now all they have to worry about is how to make huge amounts of money so that they can make the biggest, brightest and most colourful house in the neighbourhood. Families have no control over the material, labour, cost and time lines anymore. From a community effort, architecture has developed into a mere economic activity. Making a home doesn't bring the community together anymore. Lately, it has only been creating a deeper and wider crack in the society.

Is Attappady doomed now? Will our kids grow up to a land they don't identify as home anymore? Will the communities crumble into a complete void? I do see hope in the youngsters who fight against the stone quarries, sand mining and illegal logging. People are talking in dialects in public, thanks to the many efforts taken by my community as well as the various NGOs and other individuals. (In response to our request, the All India Radio created a new weekly program exclusively for tribal dialects. Dialogues and music of our homeland has been reaching the outside world through this.)

At least there is still a small minority who practice their culture including architecture, storage methods and agriculture. There are many who pass by our construction site and take time to appreciate the bamboo and mud work. Some of our friends also go outside to build with bamboo, mud, wood and steel, blending traditional and modern architecture techniques.

My family makes sure that our kids learn bamboo shoot recipes, participate in sustainable agriculture, learn to polish walls and floors with stones, learn and understand how our actions can affect everything around us and most importantly find real happiness in bonding with people and nature. We make sure that they don't miss the rich childhood that I had with tangible and intangible tech-lore. Let them get all kinds of exposure, let them choose to learn or work anywhere, and let them decide to stay or leave the village. The important thing is to keep homeland alive in their hearts. Their love for homeland should show them our planet is their larger homeland and it demands caring and sharing of space and resources. We wish that their generation grows up to be architects of life and with every new creation they build bring communities together. Human, plant or animal.

Bamboo and steel. Our latest structure. Once we have a proper wood workshop, we will be using timber rather than steel.

Volunteers repairing a check dam built with live bamboo and mud.

CRACKS AND FISSURES IN A GLISTENING TEL AVIV

Taylor Miller

I'm learning about what it means to stand with, and for, but not in place of.

By this, I mean that as a PhD student, studying the critical human geography of Palestine, I labour over what it means to practice solidarity with the Palestinian people, as well as find my own routes for standing in opposition to Israel's violent occupation of their land. What began as a project to better understand the settlement enterprise in the West Bank, specifically the behemoth land grab that is Ma'ale Adumim, has now developed into a dissertation that seeks to explicitly name, document and dismantle the neoliberalisation, gentrification and re-urbanisation of Tel Aviv - specifically through its "White City" UNESCO designation[1] and related architectural preservation, as well as the artwork and art exhibitions in the southern part of the city.

While there are more minutiae that account for this shift in research interests, I largely attribute it to a desire to understand home and the inclusions, exclusions and myriad (sometimes overlooked) violences required to stake out one's space in the city.

Tel Aviv is an ethnoreligious nationalist project with material, political and national importance to Zionist operations in Palestine.[2] The modern iteration of the city was founded in 1909 and swelled quickly as waves of Jewish European migrants arrived after WWI and WWII. Around the same time, approximately 4,000 Bauhaus-inspired and International Style buildings sprung up, mostly concentrated in the center of the city, creating a new urban core in suit with modernism's push. This white, sleek and smooth visuality lent to a global anywhereness, meaning that Tel Aviv's social space is increasingly indistinguishable from the likes of Dessau, Berlin or elsewhere in the west.

The city, designed and reproduced as both integral to the Jewish "homeland" and as a center for cosmopolitan living on the Mediterranean coast, is seldom conflated with discourses of occupied territory. Tel Aviv is far west of the Green Line[3], and internationally lauded for its quality of life, relative to other Middle Eastern cities. My digital photographs, as part of longitudinal inquiry (2014-2018), explore the cracks and fissures in such narratives of a glistening Tel Aviv. I explore this region of occupied Palestine for the ways in which the Israeli land grab exploits natural resources, dominates the built environment, yet, evidences the potentiality for colonial collapse and a reconfiguration of space that is anti-Zionist and even encouraging of Palestinian self-determination.

1. United Nations Educational, Scientific, and Cultural Organization (2018), 'White City of Tel Aviv - The Modern Movement', viewed 7 May 2018, at: http://whc.unesco.org/en/list/1096

2. LeVine, M 2005, Overthrowing Geography: Jaffa, Tel Aviv, and the Struggle for Palestine, 1880-1948, Berkeley, CA, University of California Press.

3. "The Green Line" refers to the 1949 Armistice Border, though "occupied territory" of Palestine is frequently conceptualised as the West Bank and Gaza Strip, post the 1967 war. The Balfour Declaration of 1917 and subsequent creation of British-mandated Palestine can mark the modern era of Western colonisation of Palestine. 1948 marks the Israeli Declaration of Independence, while the 1967 Six-Day War resulted in the capture of the Sinai Peninsula, West Bank, Gaza Strip, Golan Heights and Old City of Jerusalem, ushering in the contemporary era of militarised occupation.

38

סכנה
כאן בונים

MAKING OF THE MADHYA PRADESH TRIBAL MUSEUM, BHOPAL

Revathi Sekhar Kamath

All images:
Tribal Artisans at work

The Madhya Pradesh Tribal Museum, at Bhopal was commissioned in 2004 by the Government of the state of Madhya Pradesh, India. Over thirty per cent of the population of the state is tribal. The museum was designed to create a built fabric that the tribal communities could identify with, extend and evolve. It would help them to represent and express their ideas and way of life with ease and spontaneity. While the architecture of the museum was inspired by tribal rhythms, geometries, materials, forms, aesthetics and spatial consciousness, these very qualities are now acting as points of inspiration for the display of materials that are being created on-site by tribal artisans, and supported by anthropologists, sociologists and social workers.

It was important to create an architecture that was informed by the rich culture of tribal communities that have evolved over millennia. The ecology of the museum space and built form encompasses both nature and culture. The building derives its architectural expression from the metaphoric amalgam of these two elements and their balance in the physical dimension. The prime generator of form for the architecture of the museum is the quality of the topography of the region; the rolling surfaces of the Malwa plateau; rocks cupping bodies of water; gigantic steps of the Vindhya range; majestic scarps; flat topped hills dissected by several rivers and streams which run through dense forests; alluvial basins; and rocky gorges. The ensemble forms a backdrop and base for the representation of tribal habitat, stories and myths, as they unfold to a perceiver of the museum both at the urban scale and within the folds of architectural experience.

Built on seven acres, the main galleries of the Bhopal museum are raised on steel columns, forming a continuous multi-levelled verandah, following the contours of a sloping rocky terrain. The verandah manifests as a production platform where tribal artisans and artists can work in groups or individually, in a modulated space that flows into the landscape of Indigenous trees, shrubs and plants.

The rocky swales through which the rain water flows are dammed at places to create water bodies adjacent to the verandahs. Often the swales meander through the building, drawing the essential element of water inside. Court yards punctuate the expansive verandah to bring light, air and green into the space. They are placed halfway between the ground and first floor, thus establishing a spatial relationship not only with the verandah, but with the galleries and semicircular corridor.

The building's structure, inspired by the Rajwar house at Sarguja, is built from steel tubes, castellated girders, and TOR steel rods fabricated into intricate trusses. The use of steel seemed a natural choice given the placement of the museum in an area of ancient Iron and Bronze Age civilisations, the Agaria tribe, and the contemporary truck body building industry. The walls of the museum use both local stone and brick, plastered on the outside with stone dust and on the inside with mud. The ritual drawing and relief work of the various tribes rendered on the mud walls are

visually unified by the expansive use of earthy materials and elements.
The upper level of the building accommodates the entrance hall, six display galleries, a library, seminar room and auditorium. Four of the galleries are essentially rectangular and are roofed with archetypal roof configurations of the tribal buildings of the region. Two galleries negotiate the geometry of a semicircular corridor, with the rectilinearity of the galleries that are placed tangential to the curve reminiscent of the drawings of the rays of the sun in Saharia wall renderings. The human imprint on the site is carefully modulated to retain the supremacy of the prime elements (sun, air, water, earth) as well as the flow of the surroundings into and through the built form. The human influence on the project is further articulated and delineated with a hierarchy of scales into which the tribal artisans have dovetailed their skills and created nuanced overlays of consciousness.

To facilitate this independent curatorial process a number of workshops involving representative artists and artisans from different tribes were organised by the Tribal Welfare Department. Stories and myths were narrated and an inventory of different available skill sets was carried out.

As architects and conceptual interior designers, we were informed by the discussions at the workshops through which the drawings were developed. The drawings were to serve as a guideline for the coordination of the Indigenous displays in the museum's galleries. Local artists, anthropologists, sociologists and social workers were to be involved in the implementation process to guide and facilitate the tribal artisans.

The resultant design strategy generated through this consultative process suggested that the columns of the building be treated as representative of the numerous trees of the forest. The circular steel columns were worked on, with an overlay of a variety of craft skills: bamboo weaving, grass-rope work, metal and sheet metal work, wood carving, paintings etc. The corridor trusses were interpreted in different ways. The Rajwars from Sarguja recognised that steel lacing was inspired by the bamboo trusses in their own houses and therefore worked with clay figurines positioned into familiar compositions. The Bhils placed terracotta ancestral horses on the trusses and integrated them with the adjacent Pithora wall paintings, thus making the ritual paintings come alive in the space. The Baigas recreated a large tree where a truss became one of its branches. The Gonds attached wooden birds to the steel lacing. The Bharias embellished a window with carved wooden columns. In the end we found that as each set of skills found a niche for itself, the process continued to be enriched.

The four main galleries were initially conceived as representing the geographical and eco-cultural zones of Madhya Pradesh. This approach was consistently questioned by the anthropologists of the Department of Culture, who wanted a thematic representation instead. The tribal representatives present at these meetings reiterated the need for them to represent "home" and its surrounding, in these galleries. When the ownership of the museum changed hands from the Department of Tribal Welfare to the Department of Culture, the designers were persuaded to reorganise the display material into thematic headings:

- Land and People
- Living with and off the Land
- Gods
- Society and Community

The scale of the galleries was vast. To accommodate both earth and sky the ceilings were painted black to evoke a night sky and enable the display below it to be prominent and silhouetted. Large lights were placed in the ceiling and the space was flood-lit, often colouring the horizon. Dark interstitial spaces separated the exhibits. Stepped mud platforms extended the walls into the floor, creating space for a visual continuity, thus enabling a clear flow in the visual narrative.

The introduction gallery is yet to be opened for the public and regrettably our scheme for the organisation of the interiors of the gallery has been superseded by the efforts of a new curatorial team. I am told that the new team plans on placing a large mock banyan tree at the center of a map of Madhya Pradesh as the main exhibit of the gallery. The overt symbolic narrative communicated by such a piece is clearly indicative of the supremacy of the state and is represented by the canopy of the tree. Tribal culture is to be represented under the canopy. This symbolism is contrary to our set of values (developed through consultative engagement) that viewed each tribe in its ecological context. It sits in contrast to our belief that their synchronicity with natural systems and cycles hopefully become an example to support the world to evolve into an eco-literate society.

The intellectual content of the museum has certainly been compromised, but the imagery suggested in the drawings has been faithfully adhered to. Given that each individual involved has contributed creatively, we believe the museum has the strength to maintain its intellectual integrity even in the face of petty politics and bureaucratic manoeuvring. More than a thousand people have worked on the museum and the result is harmonious, not cacophonous, reinforcing my faith and belief in common consciousness.

'KIM-BARNE WADAWURRUNG TABAYL': YOU ARE IN WADAWURRUNG COUNTRY

Gareth Powell and David S Jones

We wish to acknowledge and pay respect to the Elders, families and forebears of the *Wadawurrung* peoples, the Traditional Custodians of the lands and waters that are the venue for this research and discussion, as well as Aboriginal and Torres Strait Islander peoples of the Australian continent, islands and adjacent seas, who remain the spiritual and cultural custodians of their lands and waters and who continue to practice their values, languages, beliefs and customs.

As a *Wadawurrung* man, it is my voice that narrates this article, with the respectful guidance and co-authorship of David S Jones.

This article explains the *Wadawurrung* people (the red soil people), *Wadawurrung Country*, and the dispossession of their homeland, their Country, as a consequence of European invasion of Australia.[1,2]

Wadawurrung Country consists of the lands and waters stretching from Beaufort to *Ballaarat* (Ballarat meaning "resting place" or "bended elbow"), Djilang (Geelong), Werribee (Iramoo Plains meaning "spine"), *Kuaka-dorla* (Anglesea) and the Bellarine Peninsula,[3,4] as depicted in Fig. 1.

In the beginning our Country was created by our Creation Beings who left their mark on this landscape. The *Wadawurrung* people reside on and maintain these lands and waters for sentient and non-sentient beings and their cosmos. My story of this beginning starts when *Bunjil* turned his attention to the *Wadawurrung* human creation at *Kareet Bareet* (Black Hill), near Gordon.[5,6]

In the "whitefella" beginning, "tourists" sailed passed our shores from 1421 onwards commencing with Vice Admiral Zhao Man, Flinders and Bass in 1798, and Murray entered *Nerm* (Port Phillip Bay) in February 1802. Flinders returned again in April to May 1802 mooring off Indented Head on 30 April 1802, before climbing to the top of *Wurdi Youang* (You Yangs).[7] On 1 May 1802 infamous convict Buckley camped on our Country, independent sealers and whalers camped on our shores from the 1790s to 1840s, and on 16 December 1824 Hume and Hovell entered our Country across the Werribee.

On 20 May 1835 Batman and his party sailed into *Nerm*, set up an encampment at Indented Head, and instigated our *Wadawurrung* "Invasion Day". Uninvited they assessed the agricultural economic potential of our Country before shooting a dingo without our consent, and without sensitive re-use of its carcass. Subsequently, Batman entered into a treaty with the *Wurundjeri*, our neighbours, to purchase tracts of their Country, and more significantly our Country (unbeknownst to us) for '...40

Fig. 1. Wadawurrung Country. Source: City of Greater Geelong (2016), The lands of the Wadawurrung.[20]

1. Powell, B 2015, Wadawurrung language: Kareet Bareet, Open ABC, viewed 1 January 2018, https://open.abc.net.au/explore/86715.

2. Powell, B, Tournier, D, Jones, DS, & Roös, PB 2018 forthcoming, Welcome to Wadawurrung Country, in DS Jones & PB Roös (eds), The nature of the Geelong Landscape, CSIRO Publishing, Melbourne.

3. City of Greater Geelong 2016, The lands of the Wadawurrung, viewed 1 March 2018, https://www.geelongaustralia.com.au/kaap/article/item/8d33614ddad2a9c.aspx.

4. Ibid. 2.

5. Ibid. 1.

pairs of blankets, 42 tomahawks, 130 knives, 62 pairs of scissors, 40 looking glasses, 250 handkerchiefs, 18 shirts, 4 flannel jackets, 4 suits of clothes and 150lb. of flour…'.[8]

For this treaty, the *Wadawurrung* were not invited, consulted, signatories, nor advised of this treaty making, yet it was our Iramoo Plains, *Djilang* landscape and Bellarine lands and waters that were "bought" by this land grab.[9]

Suddenly, in 1835, the shores and waters of *Nerm* were enveloped in European tourists arriving en masse accompanied by hordes of guns, wagons, sheep, cattle, seeds, pet animals, and their uncontrolled use of fire and axe. They came with a predilection to claim, conquer, fell, drain, fence and burn any Western-perceived economically prosperous land, evident in the belief that all was terra nullius.

WHAT IS WADAWURRUNG COUNTRY AND OUR COUNTRY 'DESIGN'?

To sing a narrative in *Wadawurrung* culture is to respectfully engage with my *Wadawurrung Country,* my Country, and my *Wadawurrung* identity.[10] Remember, I am talking about *Wadawurrung* Country and not any of the over 250 Aboriginal Country's across the Australian landscape, and my narrative cannot be interpreted as being the same for another Country and its peoples.

The quintessential definition of Country extensively littered in non-Indigenous publications about Aboriginal land management and Country in Australia is that offered by anthropologist Deborah Bird Rose. Rose wrote that 'Country, to use the philosopher's term, is a "nourishing terrain". Country is a place that gives and receives life. Not just imagined or represented, it is lived in and lived with'.[11]

The dilemma with this overly cited quote is that it assumes applicability to all Aboriginal Country's across Australia. And while it effectively captures a definition, this definition is becoming increasingly static. More importantly, the quotation, albeit culturally relevant and robust, is applied by students, academics and authors when they place one Country inside a box, a polygon or legally bounded space, particularly under Australian property law, and its extension into definitions of Native Title. The texts, writings, oral stories, songs and narratives about *Wadawurrung* Country should not be applied and interpreted as being applicable to another adjacent Country or a far distant Country. The quotation also fails to adequately embody the interrelationship in which Country is a place + identity + Indigenous knowledge + responsibility or obligation, and not simply place + identity.

Indigenous knowledge is located in the being that is Country. While Rose[12] talks about it philosophically, Benterrak[13] narrates the need of 'reading the Country' to experientially and physically immerse one's senses and spirituality in a place or Country. But one needs to understand that the concept of Country cannot be comprehensively translated as an environment. Powell,[14,15] explained *Wadawurrung* Country from his perspective as a *Wadawurrung* Elder, an individual *Wadawurrung* person, and a *Wadawurrung* community leader, articulating his interpretation of the translation of Country, place, meaning and relational responsibility.

So while Country may be an area of land that is overseen and managed by an Aboriginal group, like the *Wadawurrung* people, with the Creation Beings transferring *Wadawurrung* culture and language to our people, the relationship between *Wadawurrung* people and their Country extends beyond the Western sense of time. Such time is sung, is the stories embodied in and specific to Country, and is the spiritual source of knowledge essential to *Wadawurrung* past, present and future. Thus, Country is alive, intelligent and provides everything that its people need. Country exists physically outside as a living place that the *Wadawurrung* and animals and Creation Beings inhabit and is a place through which one learns culture, and gives it due regard as a template for being human in a proper and respectful way. Country provides everything the *Wadawurrung* need to equip their life, curate their land and water, feed human and animal, offer language and nomenclature as a library, and provide the operational structure to their society. For today and into the future, in anticipation of the return of their Creation Beings. It is all a design, a masterplan.

In our eyes, the landscape canvas is a product of design, hosts it and also informs it. The landscape canvas is a design historically established by *Wadawurrung* Creation Beings that both animals and humans engage with in partnership today, of which our Creation Beings established the original landscape patterns, and the rules and protocols about *Wadawurrung* Country occupancy and use.

Design is not simply about the deliverables of conventional Western briefs, but equally about individual people and animals. who design by their actions. It is also about the locus of that design. *Wadawurrung* culture exists in patterns and living conversations of relationships with our Country. Any design landscape, master plan, playground, nomenclature use, etc. needs to be informed by respectful discussions with one or more knowledge holders or Elders; not necessarily through a conventional in-room, marquee-in-the field, wander-with-an Elder, or an Elder-authored-email community engagement process.

WADAWURRUNG AS A PEOPLE AND COMMUNITY NAVIGATING CONTEMPORARY HISTORIES AND LAWS

To understand and appreciate the enormous navigational effort required to exert in relation to our contemporary histories, we have always needed to be mindful that Australia's legal system is a received system of law sourced originally and directly from English law. When my great grandfather (my mother's, mother's father) was alive, he and his parents saw first hand the effects of colonisation on my Country. It is now

6. Powell, B 2018 in press, Coolenth Jumbunna: Blackfella Talking, in DS Jones & D Low Choy (eds.), Yurlendj-nganjin: Everyone's Knowledge / Our Intelligence. Cambridge Scholars Publishing, London.

7. Powell, B 2015, Wadawurrung language: Wurdi Youang, Open ABC, viewed 1 January 2018, https://open.abc.net.au/explore/86719.

8. Batman, J 1835, The Batman Geelong Treaty, 6 June 1835, State Library of Victoria, MS13485, Viewed 1 March 2018, http://ergo.slv.vic.gov.au/explore-history/colonial-melbourne/pioneers/batmans-treaty.

9. Ibid. 2.

10. Ibid. 6.

11. Rose, DB 1996, Nourishing terrains: Australian Aboriginal views of landscape and wilderness. Canberra, ACT, Australian Heritage Commission, Viewed 1 March 2018, http://www.environment.gov.au/resource/nourishing-terrains

12. Ibid. 10.

13. Benterrak, K, Muecke, S, Roe P, Keogh, R, Joe, B (Nangan), & Lohe, EM 1996, Reading the Country: Introduction to Nomadology. Fremantle Arts Centre Press, Fremantle, W.A.

14. Ibid. 2.

15. Ibid. 6.

16. Mabo and Others v Queensland 1992 (No 2), HCA 23.

17. Australian Constitution ss 52, 90, 114, 115.

18. Australian Constitution ss 51, including its residual powers.

19. Australian Constitution ss 73, 75; Commonwealth v Tasmania 1983, 158 CLR 1.

20, Wadawarrung Country, Courtesy of City of Greater Geelong (2016), The Lands of the Wadawurrung, viewed 1 March 2018, https://www.geelongaustralia.com.au/kaap/article/item/8d33614ddad2a9c.aspx, adapted from Clark (1990).

well recorded in Australia's history that at the time of colonisation there was a choice open to the English global explorers to either: establish England's supremacy through acquisition by mutual treaty recognising the laws of the Indigenous inhabitants, or, simply and rather crudely declare the now exposed falsehood of terra nullius. They chose terra nullius as the cornerstone for founding Australia's inter-racial cohesiveness and mutually interrelated existence.

I thank God, and the bravery of Mr Mabo, along with many others who have gone before me, that the falsehood of terra nullius that the land was uninhabited was overturned by the High Court of Australia's (HCA) Mabo decision.[16] However, through the reception of English law and the process of colonisation, successive acts came into force that caused the demise and fading hope of my long lost but not forgotten ancestors. Even to this day this discourages many of my family and relatives from fully engaging with the benefits of modernity and contributing to this Commonwealth of Australia.

With the 1901 Australian Constitution enactment, an instrument that was exclusionary of the *Wadawurrung* and other tribal groups, nationally vested comprehensive powers were given into the hands of colonists, subsequent settlers and immigrants. In particular Australia's Indigenous peoples were excluded from authoritative participation in the division of powers between the Commonwealth,[17] and States.[18] We were not given standing in Section 109 of the Constitution of Australia, which gave the Commonwealth prevailing power in the event of an inconsistency of a state law and a Commonwealth law. Finally, we were excluded from full participation in the separation of powers of government: executive, legislative and judicial. In that light we were totally excluded from interpretive contributions for and on behalf of our Country, lands and waters, due to the establishment of the HCA as interpreter of the Constitution, and in 1986 as final court of appeal.[19]

With the establishment of the HCA as the final court of appeal its decisions were handed down in relation to relevant native title cases, became judge-made law as a collective body of common law, thus setting a precedent for deciding future cases with similar facts. Distinct from statutory laws or rules made by Australian parliaments, in modern context, common law comprises of the principles of law propounded by HCA judges in deciding native title cases. The good or bad effects of which are still being felt by us all.

It has now fallen to the states and territories to be extremely inclusive of our franchise as the first citizens of Australia, and as a condition of this national contract of citizenship, to see that all available means are brought to bear to enable a *Wadawurrung* voice, in the engagement with each authority under the Constitution. Moreover, for the mutually-inclusive beneficial interest in my *Country*, our great land, and the Commonwealth.

VOICE, SOVEREIGNTY AND LEGITIMACY

Our voice, sovereignty and legitimacy was set aside, but now we have returned. Since Australia's 1967 Referendum, we have progressively emerged from the depths of despair. Gathering together, settling differences amongst ourselves and other tribal groups, we do this to re-establish recognised customary boundary lines, songlines, storylines, kinship connections, and identity. Our findings from within ourselves, giving rise to our voice, our history, sovereignty and legitimacy, have increasingly unsettled established contemporary historical accounts of the *Wadawurrung* and have rewritten what it means to be Aboriginal living in modern times. I am my Country. My tribal group is my Country. My Country is us, our lands and waters.

Being a *Wadawurrung* man in these modern times, in relation to design, I am part of the masterplan created by God for the glory of His son. My Country is an expression of His handiwork, and yet I am intrinsically a living product of the fusion of both black and white worlds. Through accounts of the hardship endured by my people in previous ages, I am grateful for all the benefits which colonisation has brought to this Country. I am extremely happy to be living in this time.

Under the sovereign jurisdiction of Australia, as a legitimate Australian citizen, I am afforded state and civil protections whether individually or in business; and importantly I have the right to live. Today we have the enjoyment of machinery, education and economic progress. Today we have the right not to hunt with our spears and warrior clubs but to openly and freely explore shopping malls and the like for our food supply, clothing and necessities of life. Today we have the right to be expressive by peaceful protest against injustice; the right to freely express our religious worship.

My ancestors, along with all colonists, settlers and immigrants, would have been so much better off if Australia had not been subjected to the falsehood of terra nullius perpetrated by our nations' founding hero, Captain James Cook. All of us have suffered. Treatment of all who have opposed the Crown leading up to these modern times has been recorded as brutal to say the least. But now we move forward and what we do today is history tomorrow. In doing so, let us make that history something we may be proud of.

As we come to the end of this article I make a modern comment in relation to the notion of design and our land, our Country. We the *Wadawurrung* designed the conservation of the natural resources and economic development of our Country through the notion of measured use and preservation for successive generations. This posture is similar to what has been commonly described as environmentalism, the sustainability of the natural resources for the greater good, although it is much more than just that. However, with our consumption of globalisation, we have feasted much, and in some respects we must be mindful of past simple practices to treat our neighbour as we would treat ourselves.

As a consequence, it is important when creating or designing modern landscape apicarial (legal-religious) features and built architecture that the voice of modern *Wadawurrung* be taken into consideration as reflective of past ancestral declarations because, 'Kim-barne Wadawurrung Tabayl': You are in *Wadawurrung* Country today but you may not know it.

NOMADI/ CITY: DECOLONIAL SPATIAL PRACTICES IN NUNAVUT

Émelie Desrochers-Turgeon

Left:
Figure 02

Opposite:
Figure 04

The built environments of Inuit communities in Nunavut demonstrate that informal constructions and everyday practices reinforce a deep-rooted connection to the land.

I suggest considering those spatial practices as acts of decolonisation of the settler colonial language imposed on Inuit communities of the Canadian Arctic. Diverse modes of appropriation of settler infrastructures can be examined through the emerging material culture and construction of outbuildings and hunting cabins, as well as the appropriation of roads and government houses. Those spatial practices show the activity of groups which have to get along in a network of established forces and representations.

I propose to compare the built environments to language, which individuals and groups are given and modify. They subvert and metaphorise the dominant order, they divert it without leaving it. Those "speech acts" introduce strategies which resist a rationality, founded on notions of control and property. Based on survival, justice and self-defined work, those practices articulate an ensemble of physical places in which the energy and creativity of peoples is free to be invested meaningfully in the world. Resisting the dominance of objectivity and method, the study of Inuit cultural landscapes can use an alternative conceptual framework, opening questions about agency, performance, movement, desire, settler colonial spatial imagination and the construction of meaning.

The Nunavut territory, located in the northern part of Canada, has been inhabited by nomadic indigenous peoples, the Inuit, for over 4000 years. The establishment of Hudson Bay Company's trading posts and the arrival of missionaries from the beginning of the twentieth century influenced the permanent settlement of peoples around those trading posts. By the 1970s most Inuit families had settled and became fully sedentary, thus accessing social housing, health care, education and other services provided by the government of Canada. Nowadays the territory of Nunavut covers 2.09 million square kilometres where about 36,000 peoples[1] live, spread out in twenty-five communities[2] and whose population is very young; the median age of a resident of Nunavut is 25.1 years old, compared to that of the Canadian median of 41.2 years old.[3] Each hamlet is isolated and produces its electricity with a power plant supported by petrol. There is no underground infrastructure due to the permafrost soil; gas, water and sewage are managed by trucks travelling to every house. An annual sea lift brings food, construction material and goods to the communities; which makes the cost of living 2.2 times[4] the Canadian average. Consequently, the local dumps are widely used to find material for construction and repairs. To provide food for their community a large proportion of people hunt seal, caribou, polar bear, narwhal, fish, etc.

In short, the current model of planning of the communities in the Canadian Arctic is constituted of a complex colonial apparatus which increasingly sustains the life of Inuit people.

1. Statistics Canada, 2016 'Census Nunavut and Canda', viewed 10 May 2018, https://www12.statcan.gc.ca/census-recensement/2016/dp-pd/prof/details/Page.cfm?Lang=E&Geo1=PR&Code1=62&Geo2=&Code2=&Data=Count&SearchText=Nunavut&SearchType=Begins&SearchPR=01&B1=All&GeoLevel=PR&GeoCode=62

2. Government of Nunavut, 'Community profiles. Building Nunavut', viewed 10 May 2018, http://www.buildingnunavut.com/en/communityprofiles/communityprofiles.asp.

3. Ibid. 1.

4. Nunavut Burea of Statistics, 'Food Price Survey - Select items comparison Nunvavut Canada 2017', viewed 10 May 2018, http://www.stats.gov.nu.ca/en/Economic%20prices.aspx.

5. Baudrillard, J & Poster M, (eds) 1988, Jean Baudrillard: Selected Writings, Stanford University Press, Cambridge, Polity Press.

This apparatus ultimately aims at a form of cultural assimilation in order to inscribe bodies into the national Canadian project. The Canadian Arctic is not exactly a border, yet it is a periphery which is seen as something to be occupied in order to serve the sovereignty fantasy of what is now known as Canada.

Indeed current technocratic building practices are based upon models that often reign intellectually from top to bottom. These models postulate that space is constituted like a blank page to be written on, independent of individuals and context. Figure. 1 shows the Euro Canadian planning of the hamlet of Kanngiqtugaapik. Western preferences for Cartesian modes of practice and inquiry privilege a reductive objectivism and ocularcentrism, and the map is fraught with examples where local conditions have been overlooked in favour of accepted generalisations and top-down approaches. Cartography is a good example of this idea. Used to make "visible" what was understood as "invisible" for purposes of control, maps aim to 'create the objective space itself, open the territory, precede the territory, and rewrite the territory'.[5] Maps are meant to master an artificial language, based on a Western assumption of a "common experience". This "neutral" language rejects the local languages of the peoples and acts as a statement in support of the authority of their discourse.

As demonstrated by Figure. 1, most houses are not owned by the people who live in them, for the most part being public housing. In Nunavut, forty nine per cent of dwellings are overcrowded and/or in need of major repair.[6] These houses are mostly designed and sometimes even built in southern Canada before being sent to the communities. Not only are they poorly adapted to the local conditions but they are also clearly designed for Euro-Canadian nuclear families.

A document called 'Living in the new houses'[7] is a ninety-page guide provided in the 1970s by the rental housing program of the Department of Indian Affairs. Aiming to educate the Inuit communities to live in the new "Euro-Canadian" houses sent up north. The document explains in details the "proper" way of going about getting food, cooking, cleaning, eating, organising, storing, sleeping, washing and disposing of waste in a house. This guide, alongside the provided houses, induces behaviour in a way that controls space and time so that bodies and stories are manageable, predictable and efficient. The document illustrates racialised as well as gendered bodies in action in the domestic space. This model rests upon a Western epistemological understanding of time and space, based on function, separation, segregation and schedules; where culture is legitimised by school education that leads to wage employment and contribution to the national economy. Just as Foucault demonstrated, in a disciplinary society, apparatuses aim to create - through a series of practices, discourses, and bodies of knowledge - docile, yet free, bodies that assume their identity and their "freedom" as subjects, in the very process of their desubjectification.[8] How does one move when the city in which one lives is so different from one's traditional spatial understanding? How does one live in this settler spatial language? Where is the space of possibility?

Michel De Certeau asserts that 'the approach to culture begins when the ordinary man becomes the narrator, when it is he who defines the (common) place of discourse and the (anonymous) space of its development'.[9] Furthermore, the term "practice" is used, as put forward by de Certeau, to mean 'ways of operating or doing things'.[10] It's also understood that "spatial practices" constitute cultural practices. Merleau Ponty describes the body as "successful" when it is able to extend itself in order to act on and in the world. In the face of a colonial imposition over domestic spaces, I turn to the concept of habit to theorise not so much how bodies acquire their shape, but how spaces acquire the shape of the bodies that "inhabit" them. Presenting a few examples of overlooked qualities of built environments in Nunavut, I suggest reading those examples as acts of decolonisation of Western assumptions about space.

The proficiency of outbuildings built in between the formal governmental housing Figure. 2 demonstrates various creative endeavours in the built environment. These buildings are used as storage spaces and micro-businesses, and for repair work, workshops, artist studios, etc. These "speech acts" introduce strategies which resist a rationality founded on established notions of rights and property. Within this established place of power, the practices articulate an ensemble of physical places in which forces are better distributed and introduce a 'play into the foundations of power'.[11]

In comparing the formal road system and urban planning Figure. 1 with the actual imprint of people's circulation, either by foot, car, all-terrain vehicle or snowmobile Figure. 3, the formal road is alien to the mental geography of peoples who might privilege other means of transportation and different temporalities.[12] They represent a deep rooted nomadicity which constitutes an indigenous experience of the land based on intuition, adaptation, flexibility and movement. Even in the functionalist city, users are unrecognised producers, poets of their own affairs.

6. Nunavut Bureau of Statistics 2010, 'Nunavut Housing Needs Survey', viewed 10 May 2018, http://www.stats.gov.nu.ca/en/Housing.aspx

7. Education Branch, Department of Indian Affairs and Northern Development, 1970, Living in the new houses, Ottawa.

8. Agamben, G 2009, What is an Apparatus? And Other Essays, Stanford, Stanford University Press, pp.19-20.

9. de Certeau, M 1984, The Practices of Everyday Life, London, University of California Press, pp 24.

10. Ibid 9, pp. 11.

11. Ibid 9, pp. 38-39.

12. Ibid 9, pp. 19.

13. Rudofsky, B 1964, Architecture without Architects. A Short Introduction to Non-Pedigreed Architecture, New York, Doubleday & Company, p.6.

14. Ibid. 9, p. 40.

15. Raphals, L 1992, Knowing Words - Wisdom and Cunning in the Classical Traditions of China and Greece, Myth and Poetics, Ithaca and London, Cornell University Press, pp.12.

16. Ibid. 9, p 41.

17. Ibid. 9, pp 17-18.

18. Goeman, M 2012, 'The Tools of a cartographic poet: Unmapping settler colonialism' in Joy Harjo's Poetry. Settler Colonial Studies, vol. 2, iss. 2, pp. 101.

19. Ibid. 9. p 19.

20. Thrift, N 2009, Space: The Fundamental Stuff of Human Geography, in: Clifford N J, Holloway S L, Rice S P, Valentine G, (eds), Key Concepts in Geography, 2nd edition, London, SAGE, p 103.

21. Turner, D 2006, This is not a Peace Pipe: Towards a Critical Indigenous Philosophy. Toronto, University of Toronto Press, p. 90.

Figure 06

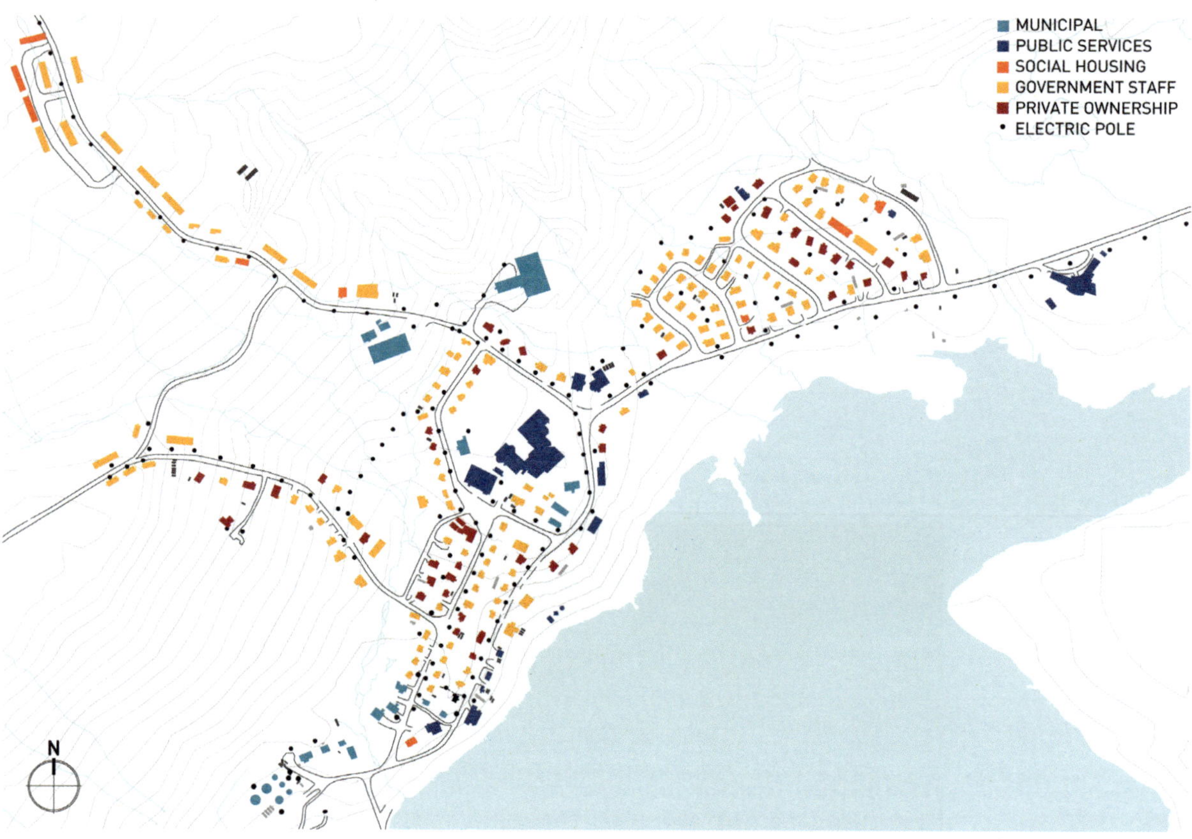

Figure 01

They trace indeterminate trajectories that do not cohere with the constructed, written, and prefabricated space through which they move. They are like unpredictable sentences within the space ordered by the organising techniques of systems. They write the rules of different interests and desires.

The hamlets' landscapes Figure. 4 are often filled with objects relating to mobility such as boats and sleds, called *qamutiks*, which are modified or built by peoples. The *qamutik*, made from recuperated or drift wood, tied together with rope, is easily repairable and responds flexibly to contact with and movement of the land, a metaphor for living in such environment. Some *qamutiks* are built as nomadic dwellings or storage devices Figure. 5, which demonstrates a concern for mobility and is reminiscent of the nomadic lifestyle.

In contrast, the current government houses use constructive detail for their foundations that demonstrate a colonial imagination. In an effort not to touch the permafrost, and to ignore the reality of the topography, there is a great distance between the ground and the floor of the dwelling. That distance makes one read the body of the house as "foreign" to the land. It acts as a rupture in the phenomenological experience of going from the land to the dwelling; now dictated by the functional infrastructure.

The foundations of cabins and outbuildings built by local communities demonstrate a renewal of the interpretation and production of these foundation systems. The foundations and floors are closer to the ground, if not touching the land. They are flexible, adaptable, low cost and low maintenance. As argued by Rudofsky, the 'untutored builders demonstrate an admirable talent for fitting their buildings into the natural surroundings. Instead of trying to "conquer" nature, as settlers do, they welcome the challenge of topography'.[13]

A common building practice consists of the building of a porch in attachment to the house. Because the government houses are placed on the land without regard for their orientation, the dwellings are modified by adding a porch to them and "correcting" the improper orientation of the doors. They also regulate the climatic differences, protect from the winds and provide important storage space for hunting tools, clothing, etc. They act as mediators between the dwelling and the land. This experience of "transition of the threshold" is crucial in the fluidity of circulation; the promenade from the inside to the outside articulates the daily experience of the land as a spatial experience based on movement and nomadicity.

The added porch, reminiscent of the traditional longitudinal threshold of the snow house, shows a formal continuity and memory of building practices. It is the presence of an absence; its traces are everywhere. The expansion of technocratic rationality has created, between the interstices of the system, an important growth of this kind of inventive practices.[14] Indeed, like improvisation made with a musical instrument, it presupposes the knowledge and application of codes which imply logic of the actions in relation to certain types of situations. The practical intelligence, defined in

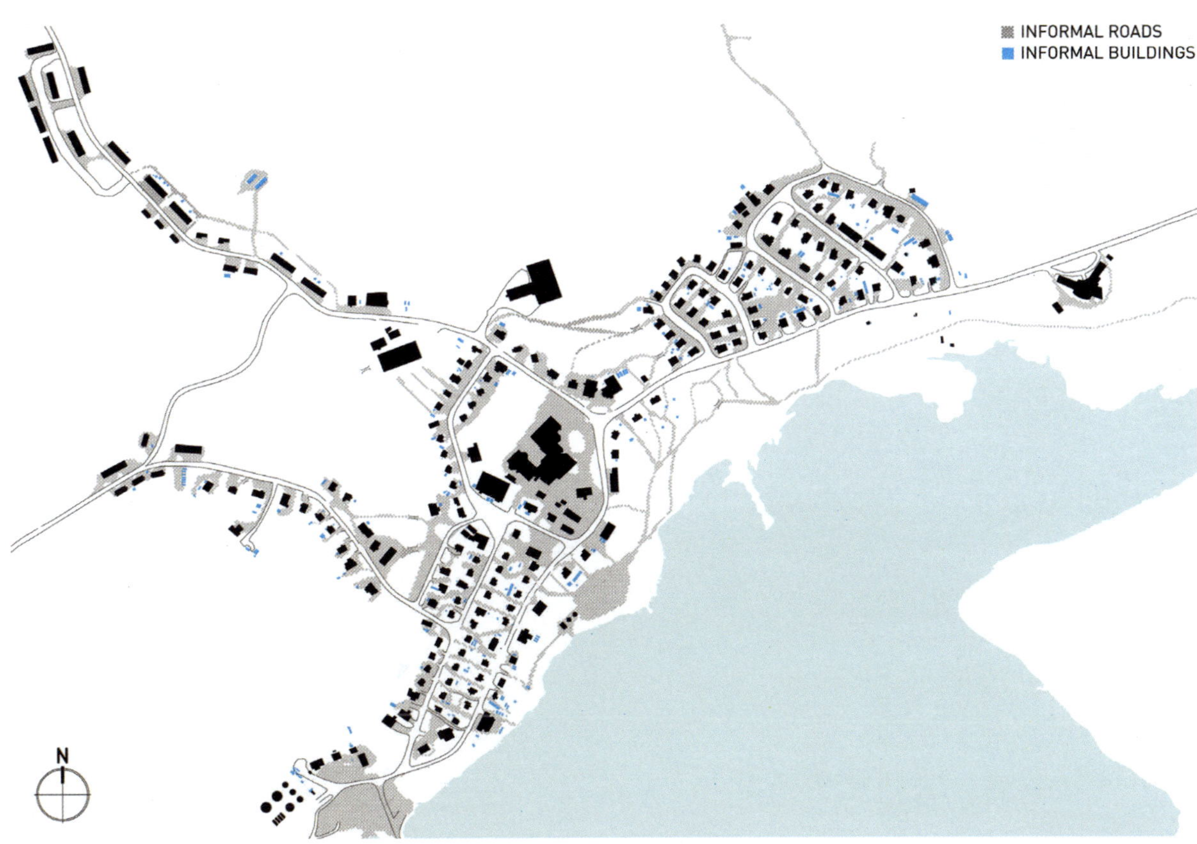

Figure 03

Greek[15] by the term *métis* suggests an alternative mode of knowing, based on "practical sense" and the "strategies" of the people.

Figure. 6 shows the materiality of a dwelling invested poetically by the act of displacing elements of the landscape - such as rocks - and to insert them on the façade of a cabin. It reflects an imagination which 'acts on the margins of a technical apparatus'.[16] People "re-employ" a system that, far from being their own, has been constructed and spread by others, and they mark this re-employment. The way they speak of this received language transforms it into a song of resistance.[17] Given the struggles and inequalities hidden under the established order, the poetic act becomes a practice which aims to make "life liveable", an art of diversion. These kinds of practices reinforce the bond of the dwelling and the land.

Mishuana Goeman wrote that 'the infinite possibility of human interaction and experience in place recalls - and, from an indigenous perspective, troubles - Michel de Certeau's concept of the "grammar of space"'.[18] She revisits Certeau's distinction between "place" as the arrangement of rules and regulations, in relationship to "space", which invokes everyday practice. She points out that the grammar of space is structured around a settler order that is inhabited, inherited, or imposed. However, this grammar is what can be play with to 'reflect "desires and goals"'.[19]

Indigenous embodied processes demonstrate how people can resist the colonial apparatuses by opening up tiny spaces. Nigel Thrift asserts that an important part of this embodied process is that 'spatial awareness we call place, which also provide cues to memory and behaviour'.[20] This study is not an attempt to codify or translate Inuit spatial languages. Its aim is not to participate in generating a discourse about Indigenous constructions but perhaps to open a window in defending the epistemological value of indigenous ways of knowing.[21]

The celebration of the agency of users can perhaps shed light on the ethical role of architects and planners and their implication in the construction of meaning and control through built environments. Until the eighteenth century, the role of architects was understood as being performative; they were responsible for the translation of ideas into the built work in situ. Today architects' role is understood as being prescriptive, through the production of highly detailed drawings.

Designers must question the role of their discipline in society; to understand to what extend design has and continues to be complicit in the colonial project is to acknowledge our inherent responsibility in designing appropriate atmospheres for human actions.

Figure 05

IN TRANSITION IS THE MOST HONEST

WINTER COUNT

WINTER COUNT is a union of artists cultivating awareness and fostering healing and protection for land and water, for all living things passed, and for all living things to come.

The growing collective of multidisciplinary artists work in film, performance, installation, sculpture, storytelling and sound composition, engaging with landscapes under current threat by extractive industry.

These conversations are ongoing, for everyone, and are accessible to the public through online platforms, museum and gallery exhibitions, screenings and public performances.

Winter Count's work has been shown at Artists Space in NYC, Center for Visual Arts in Denver, Washington Project for the Arts in Washington DC, The Museum of Capitalism in Oakland, and the Autry Museum of the American West in Los Angeles, among other online platforms, museum and gallery exhibitions, screenings and public performances.

We're witnessing natural cycles of life are disrupted by the extraction and transportation of what we have come to call resources from the land. The nations of all living things are being destroyed in this pursuit. We acknowledge that the need to protect water and land is increasing in every part of the world. As human beings, we are responsible to the ancestors and descendants of all living things for how we live. So we bring together our minds as artists to cultivate gratitude and respect for water, land, and the interdependence of all things living in this world. Through our work we bind together our diverse ancestry and cultures, to honor and protect water and land. As artists we tell stories, stories learned from each other, from land, water and all our relatives. We are listening, we are watching, we are holding up reflectors, waving flags, singing the horizon and telling the story of how we are now. As artists we are making visions and asking how we can be, what we can make for our children, and our grandchildren's children.

CAUSELINES is a project which engages a historic technology of music composition used by people of the Northern Plains.

This is a practice of studying horizon-lines from which to create melody and tone repertoire. It is a process of resonating the landscape. Binding geography to culture. Singing the song-lines of belonging. We reference this pedagogy through a confluence of newer technological platforms. We're creating scores from imagery of drone aerial footage that we have generated during times of resistance in places under threat of extractive industries: places of Cause. This imagery follows natural and human influenced landscapes; river-lines, tree-lines, road-lines, pipe-lines. These are the CauseLines from which we score. The intention of these scores is to invite processes of belonging, clarity of place. Not creating meaning but finding the meaning that already exists. The scores are to be interpreted as song, as dance, as story. It is from the complexity of interpretation, subjectivity of improvisation, that we begin dialogue around how we establish our practice of place.

In Transition Is The Most Honest

Where one thing ends and another begins,
describe the thin line of water and shore.
In transition is the most honest.
Migration is the rule of every living thing.
We have, for longer than we have been human, developed a mechanism deep in our collective brain that allows us to adapt to the changes in our environment.
We, as living things, witness the ebb of our caretaker, the earth, to teach us how to respond.
We, as living things, move as to not deplete resources.
We, as living things, shift to sustain life.
We, as living things, have always belonged to the earth.
The earth, she has shaped us, carved us from clay, sand, wood, and stone.
We are shaped by the land.
The rise of a hill in a meadow has come to shape the arch of our feet.
The overhang in a cliff the slope of our forehead.
The oxbow of rivers and the rise and fall of our breath.
Exposure to the elements has informed our form.
Salt of the sea and light from the stars has given us eyes to find our way,
our way which is not ours at all but an impulse that drives us forward into dawn.
Alas, this process of adaptation has brought us ruin as well.
Ruin in the form of gifts.
Many have forgotten their place, forgotten which lands forged their being.
The human experience is plagued by displacement.
We have an innate desire to belong to place.
This desire, this longing has been perverted to its antithesis by Western supremacy.
That creates a doctrine of discovery, eminent domain, dominion, dominance.
Where there was once use and share there is now control and subjugation.
These ideas have pushed so hard down this path that it has found its way into how we relate to one another or rather how we take and push and mine and drill into one another.
How we do this without asking? How do we tell each other that it is our fault, that we were asking for it?
And we believe and we hurt and so we hurt and hurt and hurt on a path of dependence and pity and shame.
Into fences onto farms along paths that turn to roads that run through cities and suburbs to town houses and garages, tinier still we build our world to fit us rather than adapt to fit our world.
Where one thing ends and another begins,
describe the thin line of water and shore.
In transition is the most honest.

Top:
Transition 01

Bottom:
Transition 02

Top:
Transition 03

Bottom:
Transition 04

The Firesticks Alliance Indigenous Corporation

Victor Steffansen, fire practitioner. Bundanon April 2018 mentoring in preparation for the National Indigenous Fire Workshop 2018.
Image credit: Jason De Santolo

Plants and animals have adapted over time to live with fire in the landscape. The regular use of appropriate fire on Country over time has resulted in landscapes that were, according to Captain James Cook in 1770, 'diversified with woods, lawns and marshes' and to Joseph Bank's draughtsman Sydney Parkinson, 'The country looked very pleasant and fertile: and the trees quite free from underwood, appearing like plantations in a gentleman's park'.[1] In recent times the ongoing absence of appropriate fire in the landscape has led to the bush becoming prone to wild fire, which is devastating to the ecology. Hot fires can encourage mass seed germination, which in turn creates a thick under-storey that is hard for people and animals to move through while also increasing the fire hazard through the growth of more fine fuels.

The late Kuku Thaypan Elders, Dr George and Dr Musgrave, initiated their research project in response to fires that were too hot, lit at the wrong time, in the wrong place and done the wrong way. In the words of Victor Steffensen, 'There is only one fire, and that is the right fire, for the right country.'[2] From a mainstream land and fire management perspective, this phrase 'there is only one fire' can be misinterpreted as meaning there is only one kind of fire. However, according to Awu Alaya fire knowledge there are different kinds of fire recognised in the knowledge system; each fire is considered in relation to particular qualities and needs of Country and specific conditions. Today the grandsons of Dr George and Dr Musgrave are continuing this important work on Kuku-Thaypan Country.

Unplanned wild fires and prescribed burns with hot flames can burn right up into the crown of the tree canopy. It can be very hard for the ecological system to recover after hot fires. A 'cool' fire is a preferred type of fire used by Indigenous people to look after Country. A wild fire is an unplanned fire that has a high hot flame, which burns right into the crown of the tree canopy and it is very hard for the ecological system to recover after a hot wild fire. A 'cool' fire is a preferred type of fire used by Indigenous people to look after Country. This type of flame is very low - from 1 to 2 metres. It does not get too hot, which allows the plants to recover quickly and the animals have a chance to escape or find cover in the leaf litter, in hollows of trees or underground. For countless generations Indigenous people have lived in connection with the diverse ecosystems and used this type of fire to ensure that plants, animals, birds, insects and people flourish.

WATTLERIDGE

Wattleridge Indigenous Protected Area (IPA) is situated in the temperate Northern Tablelands of NSW, covers an area of 640 ha and is owned by the Banbai Aboriginal Nation. The IPA comprises mostly granite soils supporting sclerophyll woodlands and forests[3] and is home to fifteen threatened fauna species and four threatened plant species. The Banbai rangers are managing their Country with the aim to preserve cultural and ecological values and have recently reintroduced cultural burning at Wattleridge IPA. Working with Rural Fire Services, the Banbai rangers in 2014 instituted a burning program to protect cultural sites and ensure the

Banbai rangers working in collaboration with Rural Fire Services 2014.
Image credit: Oliver Costello

land is cared for. They have commenced a collaborative research project with the University of New England in order to investigate the cultural and ecological changes associated with the reintroduction of Aboriginal cultural burning in the landscape. As part of this research, the collaborators produced *Winba* (*Winba* is the Banbai language name for fire), the Wattleridge fire and seasons calendar, which uses bio-cultural indicators to inform land managers about the changing seasons and help to guide fire management.

NATIONAL INDIGENOUS FIRE WORKSHOP: BUNDANON TRUST 2018

The National Indigenous Fire Workshop is a celebration of cultural fire knowledge and practice bringing together communities from Tasmania, Victoria, New South Wales, the ACT and Queensland. For the past nine years the National Indigenous Fire Workshops have been held in Cape York. In 2018, it was held at Bundanon Trust Reserve in Yuin Country, Southern NSW. This was an important and unique event with communities coming together over three days to continue the journey of the Cape York fire workshop series by rebuilding the fire pathways further across Country.

Bundanon Trust Reserve is a beautiful property that hosts over eleven different vegetation communities of native bushland, has an abundance of flora species and was once owned by the famous artist Arthur Boyd and his wife Yvonne. It is also the traditional home to the local Mudjingaalbaraga Firesticks team - a men's group that facilitates learning and support for men in their community and who are also leading the Firesticks Initiative in Yuin Country.

The Firesticks approach is to support Indigenous leadership through community mentorship on Country. The 2018 National Indigenous Fire Workshop fulfils the core work of Firesticks by providing Indigenous leadership, advocacy and action to protect, conserve and enhance cultural and natural values of people and Country through cultural fire and land management practices.

1. Gammage, B 2011, The Biggest Estate on Earth: How Aborigines made Australia, Allen &Unwin Sydney, pp. 5.

2. Steffensen, V 2016, Indigenous fire practitioner Tagalaka descendant, Presentation at Wujal Wujal National Indigenous Fire Workshop 2016.

3. Hunter, J 2005, Vegetation and floristics of Warra National Park and Wattleridge, Northern Tablelands, NSW. Cunninghamia, 9, pp. 255-274

4. Costello, O 2016, Indigenous fire practitioner Bundjalung Jagun, Interview Wujal Wujal National Indigenous Fire Workshop 2016, https://vimeo.com/240772284

Modern land use has made it very hard for Indigenous people to burn the land in the way that it needs in order for it to be healthy. Apart from the fracturing of Indigenous communities, with families divided and sent to other parts of the country far away from their own Country, the land itself has been fractured into many different parcels of ownership making it very difficult to look after with appropriate fire. Assets such as fences, cattle and buildings plus the variety of land tenures across a region prevent access to the land and therefore fire.

'Going forwards this is about the future of Country... It's only the beginning of a lot of hard work and a lot of responsibility, so we got to keep lighting the fires, we got to keep having the conversations, we got to keep the yarns going, and we got to keep building on the knowledge of our ancestors, the knowledge of Country. Why are we here? We got to ask ourselves that question and we got to answer it every day, we've got to get up and we got to get out there and we've got to make sure that country is looked after and that our communities are connected to each other. In the old ways people used to walk through the landscapes, we had pathways we had all these connections and everyone understood the lore. Now we don't see that and we need to see it, we need to see that lore on that landscape in that country and people looking after it.

It is so important that we maintain that connection. There is all these solutions there is all this Country that needs to be looked after and there is all these people here that want to do it together.'[4]

The Firesticks Alliance continues to actively work with communities that have regained access to their lands to treat their Country with appropriate fire. This has started the healing process for both the land and its people. Bringing people back onto Country to look after it is the first step of many that will need to be taken on the journey towards healing both land and community.

Below:
Banbai ranger Lesley Patterson shares the Winba = Fire calendar with visitors to their IPA.
Image credit: Michelle McKemey

Opposite:
National Indigenous Fire Workshop. Cape York 2014 at Steve Irwin Wildfire Reserve, hosted by Taepithiggi people, Mapoon Land and Sea Rangers.
Image credit: Jason De Santolo

NAMATJIRA PROJECT: WATERCOLOUR WINDOWS INTO PLACE

Scott Rankin

Note to the reader: I write these words, not for the Namatjira family, rather, in the context of an eight-year working relationship with them with the permission of senior family members, and to fulfil the desire of Kumatjai Mrs L Namatjira, Kevin Namatjira, Gloria Pannka and others to keep telling the story, keep making known their courage. I write with a nervousness and quiet that any sojourn into the inter-cultural domain elicits.
I fear that after eight years working with the Namatjira family, I know nothing. I fear even more that I will let my timidity cower me into saying nothing, right at the time that history demands we all speak up about our responsibilities, owning that we fail, that we make mistakes, that we stumble in our naivety, and that we can keep going together.

Australia plays host to one of humanity's greatest achievements - over 2000 generations of unbroken cultural diplomacy and ecological stewardship between Aboriginal nations and language groups across the vast Australian continent.

To put this achievement in a time-based context, Christ lived about 100 generations ago. The great pyramids were constructed about 180 generations ago. Aboriginal people have maintained a deep and continual connection to their country for around 2400 generations - 60,000 unbroken years.

Modern Australia was established by European people just ten generations ago - when *terra nullius* was proclaimed and this complex mosaic of interlinked homelands were stolen in one vast unspoken and despotic land grab. Just two generations ago, Aboriginal people were given the vote and citizenship. So this means, until two generations ago Aboriginal people - who are responsible for this incredible 60,000-year-old human achievement, were considered by white law to be part of Australia's flora and fauna.

In our contemporary, supposedly enlightened country, at the very heart of our sense of nationhood, there has been a furious peddling of deadly myths like this one, and a deliberately deceptive act of orchestrated narrative invisibility, designed to justify genocide, to substantiate the stealing of a continent, the mass displacement of people, and the suppression of the will to fight back. Internal refugees are the most vulnerable people on the planet, and Australia plays silent host to Aboriginal nations in the hundreds who have been displaced from their homelands through acts of physical and narrative violence, clumsy policy, blind ignorance and treaty avoidance. This glaringly obvious story is hidden from most Australians and sits just below the surface, infecting the soul of our country with a virulent strain of cancerous narrative denial.

To paraphrase Professor Edward Said in his book Culture and Imperialism 'nations are essentially narrations', and the invisibility of this narrative of dispossession has been maintained by deliberately excluding it from the narration that is our emerging modern nation. This dexterous vivisection of our story has rendered Aboriginal people in modern Australian society invisible in almost all major decision making and left them floundering in attempts to gain traction as something more than a footnote in this brutal rendering of historic untruths.

We may ask, what are the effects of this narrative disappearing trick? Is it just semantics, or are there consequences beyond the history books? The fact that Aboriginal people are in many hidden ways gaining, reclaiming and thriving is not a testament to the trivial effects of this narrative whitewash, rather it is an indication of the power, resilience and leadership of First Nations people across the continent.

However, this resilience sits within a context and comes from baseline of near genocide. The implications of being almost written out of the narrative are very real in the present, as any statistical analysis of social issues illustrates, whether it be health, education, infant mortality, life expectancy, superannuation, home ownership etc. Looking at youth justice for instance paints a strong picture of the implications - fifty-one per cent of the children we lock up in Australia are Aboriginal, coming from around three per cent of the population.

What then does the perpetration of this slow genocide have to do with the story of Western Aranda artist Albert Namatjira? Albert (not his real first name - adopting the name of an imperialist king who ruled over him), Namatjira (not his real surname - abbreviated), was born almost at the same moment as the federated birth of the modern nation. He walked out of his beautiful country with his parents as a toddler into Hermansburg (not its real name - named after the German town from where his missionaries came from) in 1902. He learned to walk in both worlds, and navigate the complex tsunami of change that fell upon them.

Strangely for contemporary Australians, it was much easier for Western Aranda people to understand the spiritual preoccupations and motivations of these missionaries as they looked to the unknowable spirits with new and strange forms of ritual and song and private expressions of deepening mystery and knowledge. It was much harder for people like Namatjira to conceive of the meaning behind the Whiteman's brutal new relationship to country - which allowed him talk of taking, owning, selling, fencing, and destroying country as a thing, rather than an intrinsic relationship that was full of connection and oneness, and inseparable from song, from dance, from body, from family from blood and from stewardship.

It was this relationship to country that Albert captured when he started painting with radical new technology called 'watercolour,' in the 1930s, which he learned from fellow non-Aboriginal artist Rex Battarbee. Although condescendingly accused of mimicry by some, he painted with a full awareness of the totemic power of place, and the dangers of representation. He painted with an editorial eye on keeping both the country safe, as well as the cultural safety of the uninitiated viewer. He frequently left out dangerous and sacred detail, while dexterously weaving an entrepreneurial path through technical and aesthetic considerations, sale potential, accuracy and cultural safety. In this context, what an incredible achievement each one of these pictures were, each one rare in nuance and spiritual and cultural depth. There, hidden in plain sight on every printed tea towel and biscuit tin, chocolate box and reproduced painting which adorned the walls of suburbia, was the bridging virtuosity of a man laying open his country for, in cultural safety, for these naïve European novices.

And what a pivotal function he provided, at a critical time for the emerging nation. With this outpouring of art, Namatjira opened windows of colour into alien central Australia, showing it to families huddled around the country's coastal rind - as if waiting for a ship to sail into Botany Bay and rescue them. His pictures showed them the exquisite beauty of the country that beckoned to them, that invited belonging, and offered a sense of place to these Europeans, who had blundered onto the continent, many of them refugees themselves, tired and hopeful and unaware just six generations before.

Namatjira's painting was softly cinematic, poised and alluring, as his mauve landscape spoke directly to the heart of the viewer. And in response, even as critics wavered, people flocked to his exhibitions to press red dots of enthusiastic ownership onto frames of red earth and white gums almost before they could be hung. As a result, Namatjira became rich, and at the height of his fame he was supporting 600 family members on the sales of his pictures alone, and even a young Queen Elizabeth was welcomed by a work of Namatjira and a handshake.

As the Namatjira phenomena built, he became so wealthy and important they bestowed citizenship on him. To honour him perhaps? No, so we could tax him... You can't tax a part of the flora and fauna; you can't tax an animal can you. They taxed him, but they wouldn't let him buy land. His land, in his country, that had been stolen from him.
At the height of his career, many of his fellow artists and critics couldn't see past the snobbery of their Eurocentric imperialism, dismissed him as an imitator of Western traditions - even while they themselves slavishly imitated the mediocrity of European modernity in their own work. Here was this internal refugee, this ambassador for his stolen country, this entrepreneur, this cultural innovator painting in his landscape, succeeding in both worlds, but slowly being worn down by the barbs and stick-wounds of our mindless racism. Until finally, after false imprisonment and grudging release, enough was enough, and Albert willed himself to death in his own country, the country he loved, the connection he never relinquished even in death. What was left in legacy was the sense of place he installed on countless suburban walls, which in part helped awaken a new awareness of this country, and helped break the infant teething, the Menzian bonds with the far away mother country, propelling the discussion towards citizenship, the vote, land rights, justice and hopefully constitutional recognition - all through the power of this man's attachment to country and embracing of technology.

The face of Australia internationally is, more and more that of contemporary Aboriginal art. Art that is produced in a torrent of creativity in over 100 remote arts centre across the country. These art centres are in reality "whole of community centres" supporting health and well-being, nourishment, housing, justice, transport, mental health as well as art and economic independence. And who started this art centre movement? Who got the very first art centre established? Albert Namatjira and Rex Batarbee, with Pastor Albrecht. Does our government support this vital art centre movement properly, as we exploit the imagery to push our billion-dollar tourist industry? No, of course not. We drip feed them with scattered funding, while basking in the creative glow of them internationally.

What have we done Australia? And why do we keep doing it? To listen to Albert Namatjira (real name Namatjirritja) singing on grainy film painting, singing his country as he simultaneously painted the song and the country he was painting, which was in turn his name, is to understand the privilege of living on this connected and ancient continent, and is to understand where we must try to get to as a nation. And is to acknowledge how little we know of depth in modern Australia, and how quiet we must be at a policy level while we listen for the invitation into this lovely land and complexity of place. So, let's not repeat the same arrogance and simply blame those who made mistakes in the past, let's ask anew, what is it we do not see and know... and invite instruction from elders, from place, and from landscape, as we design the narration of the nation and our future.

Albert Namatjira with wife Rubina, grandchildren and father Jonathon.
Image credit: Pastor S.O. Gross
Courtesy of Strethlow Research Centre

ENGAGING CRITICALLY

SPATIAL INEQUALITIES AND MARGINALISATION: THE BORDER-SCAPE CONDITION OF SYRIANS DISPLACED IN LEBANON

Maria Gabriella Trovato

Landscape is a complex process in which human beings and their environment are mutually defined.[1] As part of our human condition we are immersed in the environment that supports and maintains us and thus, we need to account for its continuous transformation on the basis of this immersive condition.[2] In the case of forced migration, this interrelated human/environment is roughly interrupted and messed up. The proliferation of war zones across much of the world and the consequences of climate change escalation are creating an increase in the rate of migratory flows.[3] Whole communities are forced to leave their countries to escape their places of origins. The United Nations High Commissioner for Refugees (UNHCR) Global Trends Report finds that 65.6 million people worldwide were forcibly displaced in 2016, with 10.3 million newly displaced of which 6.9 million were displaced within the borders of their own countries.[4]

Since the start of the war in Syria in 2011 more than half of the Syrian population lives in displacement within their own country or across borders seeking, asylum in the border regions. Lebanon is hosting nearly 1.2 million Syrian refugees, the largest number of refugees per capita, with one in six people being a refugee, which represents almost a quarter of the country's total population.[4]

The impact of these vulnerable displaced populations on a highly indebted middle-income country like Lebanon, resulted in a mutual and precarious crisis for both Syrian and Lebanese communities. The majority of the new displacements in 2016 took place in high-risk environments, characterised by low-coping capacity, high levels of socio-economic vulnerability, and high exposure to natural and human made hazards.[5] This continuous flux and movement of people is determining new spatial dynamics and social geographies.[2] Relocated in different context, displaced communities are re-shaping the physical and temporal processes of the land, establishing new relations (Fig. 1) between the existing and the newly-inserted, informal structures. Over time, these migrations are making over the morphological organisation of the land, generating new geography patterns marked by materiality, leakages and practical enactments of border-scape practices.[6] This investigation into the border condition of the spatial organisation of displaced Syrians' flow, within urban and rural context, aims to depict the magnitude of the phenomena, while treating the borders as a complex spatial devices, reveals ways of defining and handling space and time in an uncertain and informal condition. Meanwhile, this investigation aims to represent the palpable fluidity and evolution of the displayed condition by looking at "human action" as a significant component of a site and important shaper of the contemporary landscape.

1. Menatti, L 2017, 'Landscape: from common good to human right', International Journal of the Commons, vol. 11, no 2, pp. 641–683.

2. Barnett, R 2013, Emergence in Landscape Architecture, Routledge, London.

3. Sassen, S 2016, A Massive Loss of Habitat, Sociology of Development, vol. 2 no. 2, pp. 204-233

4. UNHCR Global Trends 2017, 'Forced displacement in 2016', Geneva, viewed 10 April 2018, http://www.unhcr.org/5943e8a34.pdf.

5. Internal Displacement Monitoring Center (IDMC), 2017, Global report on internal displacement in 2016, Geneva, viewed 5 April 2018, http://www.internal-displacement.org/global-report/grid2017/pdfs/2017-GRID.pdf .

6. Fawaz, M 2017, 'Planning and the refugee crisis: Informality as a framework of analysis and reflection,' Planning Theory, vol. 16 no. 1, pp. 99–115, viewed 10 April 2018, http://journals.sagepub.com/doi/pdf/10.1177/1473095216647722.

7. Brambilla, C 2015, 'Exploring the critical potential of the borderscapes concept', Geopolitics, vol. 20, no. 1, pp. 14-34.

Figure 02. Landscape inequalities are exacerbated by the multplication of border demarcations, and denial of access to infrastructure and landscape resources.

Limitations in this research arose from the complexity and magnitude of the phenomena, the multiplicity of experiences, the political/religious implications, and the presence of multiple local and international actors, who are often mistrusted by the displaced community; and the difficulty in monitoring these changes through time due to the dynamic and ever-evolving situation.

Displaced Syrians constitute a marginalised population defined in relation to the specific characteristics of the country in which they now find themselves and to the war in their homeland. Challenges associated with these definitions impede the ability of Syrians in Lebanon to take collective action in relation both to their own security and other aspects of everyday life.[7]

In Lebanon, a city's ability to absorb the very large numbers of refugees rests on the flexibility and responsiveness of informal housing markets (Fig. 5), which react resiliently and promptly to the spike in demand.[8] Syrians are organised largely in relation to the local structures and networks of Lebanese society, but on its margins. Landscape inequalities are exacerbated by the multiplication of border demarcations, and denial of access to infrastructure (Fig. 2) and landscape resources. The border remains important to both host and hosted populations as they confront accelerating social change unleashed by the crisis, and restricts Syrians to the role of outsiders. They are totally isolated in their social and political marginalisation.[7]

Forced to abandon their familiar landscapes and cultural comfort zones, and feeling out of place both physically and socially, displaced Syrians experience a traumatic relocation. Their accommodation in inadequate, and overcrowded built structures alters their spatial experience by restricting them to a severely closed and limited physical place. These hardships, affected by spatial conditions and access to spatial resources, as well as affecting potential positive associations with landscape, are at the core of landscape justice.[9]

This investigation showed that life in the unfinished Informal/illegal settlements in the Lebanese urban and peri-urban areas is a struggle between the desire to return home, given the transitory nature of the refugee settlements, and the attempt to create a sense of stability to be able to engage in daily activities.

The Ouzai building is a structure located at the outskirts of Saida, Lebanon. It was meant to become a campus for the Al Iman Al Ouzai University, but an agreement between the Islamic Education Center, the UNHCR and Premiere Urgence-Aide Medicale Internationale allowed displaced Syrians to locate there, transforming the building in a small city. Between 120 and 175 families, mostly from the same village in the fertile plains of Hama in western Syria, live in large family units with around ten children per family and an estimated population ranging from 900 to 1500. The progressive shaping and re-adaptation of the inside space of this built structure testify the inhabitants' effort to reproduce the residential fabric of their original villages with their socio-spatial organisation and division between public and/or private, open and/or closed.

Ephemeral landscapes emerge at various times of the day before disappearing without leaving material traces of their existence. Permanent signs of appropriation are present wherever there is too little privacy, and open spaces represent a danger to the respect and visibility of intimacy. Protection elements (Fig. 10) start from narrow interiors and arrive at the threshold to prevent passers-by from getting too close to the intimate space. The limit defines the extension of familiar territory. Its mark designates a possession and the possibility of claiming a right.

The relocation of millions of individuals from their territory of origin, whether it is the result of coercion or free choice, determines a "de-territorialisation of culture" and the end of the equation of culture, territory and identity, which, until recently, was considered the salient component of the existence of community.[10] This research is based on the assumption that people who are forced to give up a landscape and move to create a home elsewhere, are likely to reinterpret old landscape values in different locations and to remold the new landscape to reflect those values. Thus, landscape knowledge is transported, and new landscapes are created in the attempt to reestablish lost connections and to redefine a sense of belonging. The results of this study, while not exhaustive, present a situation in which scattered but numerous new cultural identities affect and transform the landscape by creating new ones from the addition and overlapping of local and imported models. The focus on the borders, regarded as socio-cultural and discursive processes and practices, highlights the different spatial practices implemented by displaced communities to recreate places (Fig. 03). Because "place" is an important aspect of human existence, and it is an important source of security and identity. Places shape our memories and feelings (Fig. 02), and in turn people shape the landscapes around them based on their experiences and actions.

8. Boustani, M, Gebara, H, et al 2016, 'Beirut, a safe refuge? Urban refugees accessing security in a context of plural provision', UNHABITAT report, viewed 15 April 2018 http://unhabitat.org/beirut-a-safe-refuge-urban-refugees-accessing-security-in-a-context-of-plural-provision/

9. Egoz, S, & De Nardi, A 2017, 'Defining landscape justice: the role of landscape in supporting wellbeing of migrants, a literature review', Landscape Research, vol. 42, supp. 1.

10. Fabietti, U 2015, Nel traffico delle culture/in the traffic of cultures, Lotus International, 158, pp. 89-99

Figure 03. The focus on the borders highlights the different spatial practices implemented by displaced communities to recreate place.

Figure 01. Displaced communties are re-shaping the physical and temporal processess of the land.

DARK LANDSCAPES: INTERPRETING THE KILLING TIMES

Robyn Smith

Sites of death, suffering and the macabre that have become tourist attractions fall into a category known as "dark tourism".[1] An endless list of sites comes to mind at home and overseas, perhaps most famously Rome's Colosseum, the Egyptian Pyramids, Auschwitz, prisons and psychiatric institutions.

Arguably Australia's highest profile dark tourism site is the $100 million Sir John Monash Centre at Villers-Bretonneux, officially opened on ANZAC day 2018 and hailed by the Daily Telegraph as 'a triumph' of Prime Ministers John Howard, Tony Abbott and Malcolm Turnbull.[2]

Let's consider the notion of the "dark landscape", hitherto a term reserved for artwork titles. The dark landscape, a new term attributable to sites of massacres, is a site of death, suffering and the macabre, but not necessarily one that has been marked or interpreted and is certainly not a tourist attraction. In stark contrast to the Monash Centre there are few tributes - and no comparable expenditure - put toward the countless dark landscapes at home, the sites of frontier warfare and massacres across the Australian continent. Largely ignored, these sites require a new, intelligent and innovative approach to interpretation. They are sites of bloodshed and loss, of tragedy and injustice. They should be memorialised not in the colonial tradition of a white man chiselled in marble, elevated and lording it over everyone else in a nod to British social hierarchy, but in a way that is representative of the egalitarian Aboriginal cultures that were so severely affected by them; they should be places of reflection and contemplation, like the Sir John Monash Centre.

Given that many Aboriginal cultures are so intrinsically linked to nature, landscaping is one way of providing appropriate interpretation of the sites in a nod to traditional practices of caring for Country and passive, rather than rigidly instructive, learning.

Interpretation is not without its difficulties. Aslan warned:

> ...dark tourism sites present governments and other authorities with moral and ethical dilemmas, where recent tragic history often confronts the dynamic of commercial development and exploitation. These dilemmas include depicting and managing the often-contentious past. Commemoration of events and practices can also be manipulated for political reasons.[3]

That notwithstanding, dark landscapes provide a rich palette because these sites run all the way from the Top End of the Northern Territory to almost the southern tip of Tasmania. While there are issues of climate and botany, some sites pose the more challenging issues of remoteness, visitation and management.

Take, for example, the site of the 1928 Coniston Massacre in the Northern Territory. At Coniston Station in Central Australia a dingo trapper, Frederick Brooks, was murdered by Aboriginal people.[4] The facts of the case are disputed. The retaliation that followed was sanctioned and merciless. The number of Aboriginal people killed is not known, although the official figure was thirty one some historians, such as Dick Kimber, put the number at two hundred.[5] Wilson and O'Brien have 'information derived from actual perpetrators that the total Aboriginal death toll was at least twice the official figure'.[6] This was not a single massacre in a single place; it covered significant distances over a period of weeks.[7] It is quite clear that poor records, lack of government interest, secrecy and denial meant accurate numbers were rarely available following massacres. In the oral histories of many Aboriginal language groups, such encounters are recalled as 'the killing times'.[8,9,10]

Coniston was home to the Warlpiri, Anmattyre and Kayete people. It is arid land and, in 1928, was coming off a four-year drought. Few people live there now[11] because pastoralists abandoned it and, during and after the massacre, Aboriginal people fled to 'a great circle of sanctuaries', notably the communities of Lajamanu, Kalkarindji, Tennant Creek, Alekarenge and Yuendumu.[12] Lajamanu (formerly known as Hooker Creek) and Kalkarindji (formerly known as Wave Hill) are to the west of Katherine in the Top End; the remaining communities are in Central Australia. The diaspora is vast. Read and Read noted: 'Sixty years after the Coniston Massacre many of the elderly still found it too sad to return to the Warlpiri heartland'.[13]

Coniston does not sit in isolation. There were innumerable massacres throughout Australia, most of which have yet to be acknowledged or, just as importantly, interpreted. It is convenient to suggest that interpretation be of the traditional colonial type – typically a statue or museum. Both are built structures and neither conform with local Aboriginal cultural practices including, for some groups, avoiding the likeness of a person person after their death (statue, photograph) and, in the case of some nations in the Northern Territory, not uttering the name of a deceased person (museum, exhibition, place named after an individual) until family has declared that the appropriate mourning period has passed.[14] These places are about the collective and while they present unique challenges, there is an equally unique opportunity to apply creative and meaningful design to sites comprised of an imperative, but largely untold, chapter in Australia's history.

The International Council on Monuments and Sites' ICOMOS Charter for Interpretation and Presentation of Cultural Heritage Sites[15] sets out seven principles:

1. Access and Understanding:
Facilitate access for all.

2. Information Sources:
Ensure interpretation is scientifically based.

3. Context and Setting:
Relate interpretation to wider context and settings.

4. Authenticity:
Respect traditional social functions.

5. Sustainability:
Implement effective strategies for economic, environmental and social sustainability.

6. Inclusiveness:
Involve all stakeholders in the development of interpretive programmes.

7. Research, Training and Evaluation:
Implement technical and professional standards in interpretation.

Access and understanding gives rise to the potential for virtual interpretation, particularly sites that have been built upon or are in very remote regions that are unlikely to attract large visitor numbers, which reduces the potential for education. With the growing number of massacre sites identified in Australia it is perhaps not physically possible to mark and commemorate them individually. This doesn't negate the need for detailed holistic interpretation and, of course, interpretation of individual sites where it is possible to do so. Clearly, this requires the consent and input of Aboriginal survivors and/or descendants.

Thanks to the work of the team at the Centre for 21st Century Humanities at the University of Newcastle[16], there is a growing body of information sources in relation to massacre sites around Australia. It is important to remember here that there are often conflicting histories about what happened. It is also critical that all of the available information is used to appropriately interpret sites to provide the most accurate understanding of events.

In many Australian Indigenous cultures, artwork, oral stories, song lines and gatherings are important sources of information and ways to commemorate events. In one case at least there is a corroboree[17] recounting the successful repulsion of attempted settlement at Fort Dundas in the 1820s on the Tiwi Islands to Darwin's north.[18]

The third principle, context and setting, provides the opportunity of interpreting a site as a natural, rather than predominantly built, monument. It is consistent with caring for Country and leaving land as undisturbed as possible so it can regenerate and provide during the next season. Indeed, in the case of frontier massacres, it was often competition for natural resources that gave rise to conflict.

It may be that a site includes a coastal area where there is a reef or cliffs that were used as rock pools for fish traps. If these geological features remain they can, and should, be incorporated in the interpretation.

Location of the site will be critical to application of the authenticity principle. If the site is now in an urban setting, preserving its original authenticity will be difficult and must take into account the evolution of the place over time, but this is not insurmountable and adds to the accuracy of interpretation.

In some cases, environmental sustainability may present a challenge. For example in arid areas or those suffering drought conditions, reticulation will be required to preserve an interpreted dark landscape. Use of native flora will assist, but droughts pose a threat and should be considered during the planning stage. Similarly, sites involving cliffs where there are rock falls might be challenging, however a dark landscape interpreted away from the cliffs while retaining them clearly in the line of sight would appropriately address the issue.

1. Aslan, S 2015, 'Prison tourism as a form of dark tourism', Journal of International Social Research, vol. 8, no. 40, pp. 600 - 608.

2. Divine, M 2018, Daily Telegraph, 'Villers-Bretonneux WWI memorial is a triumph', viewed 28 April 2018, https://www.dailytelegraph.com.au/rendezview/villersbretonneux-wwi-memorial-is-a-triumph/news-story/40cf0e30229cf259f6b817db167384b7.

3. Ibid. 1.

4. Smith, R 2013, Two men, Padygar and Arkikra were twice tried and acquitted of the murder', in Antecedents: The History of Ward Keller, Ward Keller, Darwin, pp. 31 - 32.
5. Wilson, B, O'Brien 2003, 'To infuse a universal terror: a reappraisal of the Coniston killings', Aboriginal History, vol. 27, pp. 59–79.

6. Ibid. 5.

7. Ibid. 5.

8. Read, P and J (Eds) 1991, Long time, olden time: Aboriginal accounts of Northern Territory history, Institute for Aboriginal Development Publications, Alice Springs.

9. Oral history from: Cribbin, John 1984, The killing times, Fontana/Collins, Sydney.

10. Jampijinpa Brown, W 2013, Warlpiri Drawings; 'Killing Times' at Coniston', National Museum of Australia, viewed 1/5/2018, <http://www.nma.gov.au/exhibitions/warlpiri/works/coniston>.

11. In 2014, a land title of one square mile was handed over to traditional owners at Yurrkuru, 275km north-west of Alice Springs.

Inclusiveness may be useful for an overview of dark landscapes across Australia to illustrate the number of known massacres, the geography over which they occurred and the range of habitats in which they occurred, from northern coastal to inland arid, temperate and cool-temperate regions. A common theme giving rise to competition for resources was water.

The research, training and evaluation principle cautions against a one-off interpretation and then leaving the site as completed. ICOMOS recommends constant reassessment, evaluation and ongoing interpretation of a site as either the site evolves, or new information comes to hand. This principle also encompasses international cooperation and the sharing of experiences. For example, how massacre sites are presented and interpreted in former British colonies such as New Zealand and Canada.

History is not always pretty. That doesn't mean it should be ignored. Nor does it mean that all history should be treated in like manner. Statues and monuments are not appropriate for the interpretation of Aboriginal cultures generally, and certainly not for the interpretation of massacre sites. Interpretation of these dark landscapes requires fresh eyes and innovation combined with respect for Indigenous First Nations cultural traditions and land management practices.

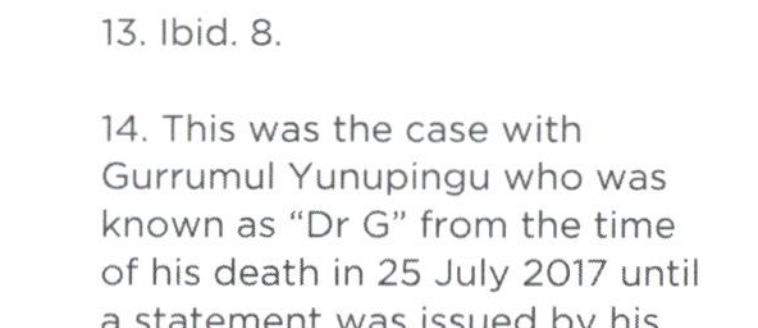

12. Ibid. 8.

13. Ibid. 8.

14. This was the case with Gurrumul Yunupingu who was known as "Dr G" from the time of his death in 25 July 2017 until a statement was issued by his family on 20 December 2017. This is a relatively short period; usually the length of the observance is determined by the seniority of the person concerned.

15. International Council on Monuments and Sites (ICOMOS) 2008, The ICOMOS charter for the interpretation and presentation of cultural heritage sites, viewed 1 May 2018, https://www.icomos.org/charters/

16. University of Newcastle 2017, 'Colonial frontier massacres in central and eastern Australia 1788-1930 map', Centre for 21st Century Humanities, viewed 1 May 2018, https://c21ch.newcastle.edu.au/colonialmassacres/.

17. Similarly, there is a corroboree recounting the Tiwi experience of the Bombing of Darwin. This is known as the 'aeroplane dance'.

18. Poignant, R 1996, 'Ryko's photographs of the 'Fort Dundas riot': the story so far', Australian Aboriginal Studies, No 2, pp. 24-41

Top Figure, 01:
Tiwi Islanders using spears as firearms in the Fort Dundas Corroboree. Photograph by Ted Ryko, 1914-17. Image credit: Northern Territory Library.

Bottom, Figuore 02:
Coniston Station Homestead, 1928
Image credit: National Archives of Australia.

Opposite, Figure 03:
2011 – Remembering the directions in which people fled from Coniston by Ruth Napaljarri Oldfield, Yuendumu
Image credit: AIATIS Collection

ANCIENT INNOVATIONS: FROM THE FOURTH TO THE FIRST WORLD

Julia Watson

'Every culture is by definition a vital branch of our family tree, a repository of knowledge and experience, and, if given the opportunity, a source of inspiration and promise for the future.'
Wade Davis, The Wayfinders.

Conservation has failed us. At the time of its birth in the 1800s, Darwin's thinking dominated scientific discourse with evolutionary theories like 'the survival of the fittest' and 'extinction happens slowly'.[1] In the past fifty years we've lost over half of the world's biodiversity[2] and have entered a period of mass extinction that threatens humanity's existence. Conservation can't save us. It was conceived to preserve and protect America's wildlife and wild lands, offering respite and recreation for city dwellers. As we confront the reality of a world facing extreme climatic change and rapid species extinction caused by our failure to protect the natural systems that sustain our existence, it becomes apparent a paradigm shift is required. We need to rethink our approach from the ground up. Reflecting contemporary ecological thinking, a shift in our perception from 'survival of the fittest' to 'survival of the most symbiotic', is a critical first step.[3]

Fourth World people, who are hunter-gatherer, nomadic, pastoral and subsistence farming peoples, living beyond the modern industrial norm,[4] are the principle protectors of the world's biodiversity and instrumental to the success of a new model for conservation. The protection of the global Shadow Conservation Network, the informal network of Indigenous lands, will become critical in the fight against extinction. While today we recognise that Fourth World people play a critical role in saving global biodiversity, this has not always been the case. In the shadows of the conservation movement lies a secret story of displacement. Over one million conservation refugees,[5] mostly Indigenous people, have been displaced from their native lands in the creation of conservation areas. Accompanying this mass displacement is the destruction of ecologically intelligent infrastructure and the loss of traditional ecological knowledge that has fostered symbiosis between human and non-human species. At the time of its conception, the forefathers of conservation did not imagine that their movement would lead to the displacement of millions of people and accelerate the global loss of biodiversity to such a degree that it would counter their core mission. Rather than protecting the wild, in some cases conservation has displaced it, leaving us with a legacy of loss.

Across the world, hundreds of millennia-old, man-made innovations exist. These local ecological adaptations - ancient innovations - are designed in response to environmental crisis such as famine, flood, drought, storm, lack of territory or arable terrain. Fourth World people[6] construct infrastructures to overcome environmental obstacles. Indigenous innovations offer many unique ways of living symbiotically with nature. This article explores the Indigenous infrastructures of the Fourth World and builds an argument towards their documentation, adaptation and potential reapplication. Guided by three questions, this article investigates the material, module and system scale of physically similar but geographically distant ancient innovations, and presents them through an architectural lens.

1. What sustainable knowledge do Fourth World people know that we once knew?

2. Is this knowledge lost or just forgotten?

3. How can designers use this knowledge today?

From floating islands in southern Iraq to forest agriculture in Brazil, ancient innovations have not been forgotten but rather are hidden, in some of the most remote places on earth.

Living in the harshest and most vulnerable places, Fourth World people exist in self-sufficient units, solving environmental challenges by applying Traditional Ecological Knowledge[7] (TEK). TEK is a field of study in anthropology defined as a cumulative body of knowledge, practice and belief, handed down through generations by traditional songs and stories. It describes Aboriginal, Indigenous, or other forms of traditional knowledge that sustain local resources. TEK is acquired over hundreds or thousands of years through direct contact with the environment by adapting natural systems into Indigenous infrastructures at vast scales. Rather than exploiting their environments, Fourth World people are natural system engineers.

This article begins to build a compendium of Indigenous infrastructures that showcase the biodiverse environments and infrastructures humankind is capable of creating. Included in a forthcoming book are case studies of the following communities; the Kayapo of the Amazon Basin; the Chagga at the base of Mt. Kilimanjaro in Tanzania; the Masaai and Turkana of Kenya; the Uros of Bolivia; the Ma'dan of southern Iraq; the Subak of Bali; the Ifugao of the Philippines; the Khasis of northern India; the Enawene Nawe of Brazil; the Incas of Peru; the Maya of Mexico; the Javanese of Indonesia; the Ma'dan of the southern wetlands of Iraq; the ancient Persians of Iran; the Malayali of India; the Zuni of Mexico; Tofinu of Benin and the Bengalese of the East Kolkata Wetlands of India and the ancient innovations found there. This survey will showcase the complexity of ancient innovations in existence today, reframing the paradigm of the Fourth World as "primitive", to that of innovative.

During the Age of Enlightenment, humanity defined technology. Of all the local innovations that existed in the world at that time, only a sliver originating in the West, was deemed valuable and shepherded through to the present day. This worldview has dominated our technological thinking, distanced humankind from nature, and led us to our present environmental predicament. As designers in the era of the Anthropocene, we've inherited an unknown environmental legacy. While we have to do things differently, we don't know how.

Universally the forces of colonialism, capitalism and conservation have dismantled local innovation and left our environs littered with failing infrastructures. We confront climate crises armed with a limited palette of scalable and sustainable strategies. Borne out of scarcity, a necessity for sustainability, adaptability and resilience, Indigenous infrastructures from the Fourth World offer alternative solutions for designers confronting climate change. These innovations dispute the perception that Indigenous peoples are frozen in a pre-modern time, existing isolated from technology. Rather than seeing the Fourth World as impoverished, with little innovation to offer, this article views Indigenous infrastructures as sophisticated technologies, ranging in size from river crossings to watershed reconstructions. Fourth World peoples are accomplished innovators, armed with Traditional Ecological Knowledge that has guided them for millennia.

Independently evolved but similar innovations are a reoccurring phenomenon found across the globe. Isolated communities living in similar biomes and contending with similar constraints autonomously arrive at the same solution. This contends that certain problems precipitate optimal solutions to constraints such as the use of pyrotechnology to generate forest-farming systems from nutrient deficient soils or the construction of freestanding, mortar-less, walled fish traps in the intertidal coastal zone.

Pyrotechnology is a global phenomenon used as a tool in farming adopted by the Mardu people of Western Australia, the Milpa of Mesoamerica, the Chagga of East Africa, the Kayapo of the Amazon Basin and the Anishinaabe of northern Canada.[8] In the sacred mythology of the Anishinaabe people, a mythological creature called the Thunderbird shoots lightning or puhkeenun by the blinking of its eye to begin the seasonal spring fires that renew the vestiges of the winter.[9]

Ancient folklore explains that when the ice on a lake turns from cloudy to clear and begins to break, it's time to light the seasonal spring fires.[10] The Anishinaabe have learnt to control the spread and heat of fire to diffuse potential destruction. Fire allows the new passage of wind to reduce mosquito infestation and stimulate new growth for habitat, insulation, housing and bedding. With a deep understanding of the life cycle of successional growth that occurs after fire, new productive forest ecosystems are possible. For example: blueberry patches spontaneously grow and attract larger animals to hunt.[11] (Fig. 01)

Similarly, in Mesoamerica pyrotechnology is an operation used to create new successional ecosystems. The forest-dwelling Kayapo people practice shifting cultivation, which is a type of farming that begins with slash and burn. It begins when an area of jungle is cut down and burned to cultivate the soil in preparation of an Apete forest farming village that will be grown in its place. In close proximity, the Milpa is an ancient Mayan intercropping system planted in the forest, which uses pyrotechnology to build biodiversity by succession. It is composed of "The Three Sisters"; maize (corn), beans and squash, which have been the principal diet for the Mayan civilisation for millennia. This system of planting is found in several different Indigenous nations (Mayan, Aztec, Pueblo, Anasazi, Tewa, Cherokee and Iroquois), which is testament to the efficacy of grounding this framework of understanding in a familial mythology. (Fig. 02)

From origin stories to everyday life, maize and humans have formed a deep spiritual connection over thousands of years. In Mayan mythology the first mothers and fathers of the Maya were formed from maize,[12] so the practice of Milpa is a responsibility given by the gods. Legend tells that the white corn formed their bones, yellow corn their flesh, black corn their hair and eyes, and red corn their blood. Milpa plantations are thus believed to be places of spiritual significance, and the cultivation of maize is considered a spiritual act.[13] Many ceremonies are still carried out as part of the annual agricultural cycle of Milpa, from soil preparation to harvest.

For people living on reef systems, the land-sea interface is adapted to provide communities with resources such as food, building materials, medicines and firewood, while also offering coastal protection from storm and flooding events, biodiversity conservation and integrated ecosystem management.
On isolated islands across the Pacific, ancient innovations stretching from forest to foreshore like the ahupua'a of Hawaii, the vanua of Fiji, the subak of Bali and the derderin of Australia are composed of cooperative land division and adaptive management systems.
A key feature of the vanua and the ahupua'a are the intertidal aquaculture

1. Darwin, C and Wallace, A 1859, Origin of Species, London, John Murray.

2. McRae L, Freeman R, & Deinet S 2014, 'The Living Planet Index' in McLellan, R, Iyengar, L, Jeffries, B and Oerlemans, N (eds), Living Planet Report 2014: species and spaces, people and places, Gland, Switzerland.

3. Margulis, L, 1998, Symbiotic Planet: a New Look at Evolution, Basic Books.

4. Manuel, G 1974, The Fourth World: An Indian Reality, New York, Free Press.

5. Dowie, C, 2011, Conservation Refugees: The Hundred Year Conflict Between Global Conservation and Native People. Boston, MIT Press.

6. Manuel, G 1974, The Fourth World: An Indian Reality, New York, Free Press.

7. Berkes, F 2012, Sacred Ecology: Traditional Ecological Knowledge and Resource Management. Philadelphia, Taylor and Francis.

8. Ibid 7.

9. Miller A & Davidson-Hunt, I 2010, 'Fire, Agency and Scale in the Creation of Aboriginal Environments', Human Ecology, June, vol. 38, no. 3, pp. 401- 414.

10. Ibid 9, pp. 401-414

11. Ibid 9, p. 401.

12. Tedlock, D 1996, Popol Vuh: The Mayan Book of the Dawn of Life and the Glories of Gods and Kings, New York, Touchstone.

13. Frece, A & Poole, N 2008, 'Constructing livelihoods in rural Mexico: Milpa in Mayan culture', The Journal of Peasant Studio, vol. 35, no. 2, pp. 335-352.

14. Ibid 7.

ponds, which are similar in design to the ponds built by the Lardil people of the North Wellesley Islands in Australia. Freestanding mortar-less rock walls, which begin on coastal land and extend out to sea, are built to flood, then trap sea animals over the course of a tide. Through the high tide walls will submerge, but as the water recedes with the low, sea life is trapped. This ancient innovation allows for selective fishing, prevents overharvesting, and protects threatened species.

Constructed without mortar, some freestanding rock traps date back 500 years. The Lardil people take advantage of oyster colonies that stabilise the walls with calcium carbonate as they attach to surfaces between rocks that provide an ideal habitat for colonisation. The sandy or muddy seafloor stabilises the rocks aided by mangrove roots that entwine within the walls, taking the impact of tidal force. The derderin aquaculture system developed by the Lardil people evolved a symbiotic relationship between oyster colonies and rock walls by offering habitat which provides structural integrity to the overall construction. Both the exploitation of symbiotic relationship and the principle of similarity in basic design but difference in deployment based upon localised conditions replicates globally, varying according to topography, materiality and species endemism.

The core characteristics of ancient innovations embody the key principles of resilience thinking and their potential for replicability is the most exciting and impactful opportunity for designers addressing climate change. While largely undocumented and unknown to designers these systems have been studied by ecologists and anthropologists. Design is at a pivotal moment. As designers, we are expanding the field to confront complex problems

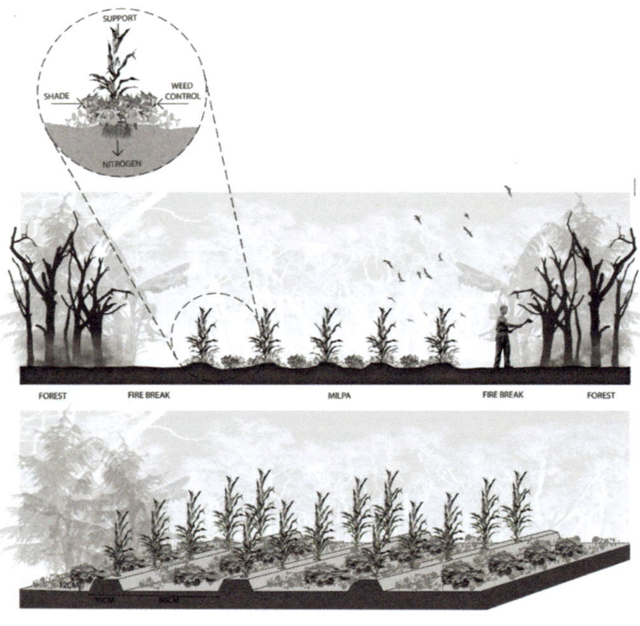

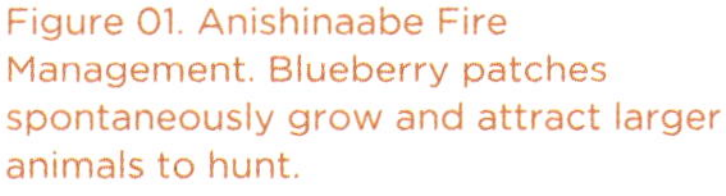

Figure 01. Anishinaabe Fire Management. Blueberry patches spontaneously grow and attract larger animals to hunt.

Figure 02. Milpa: Ancient Mayan intercropping system planted in the forest, which uses pyrotechnology to build biodiversity by succession.

that require robust and adaptive responses. It's critical to arm oneself with new knowledge and tools that expand our understanding of infrastructure and the design of complex natural systems in a multitude of contexts.

As mentioned by Fikret Berkes and supported by historical studies,[14] the potential to migrate these ancient innovations to similar biomes exists. In the case of the *qanat*, which is an underground aqueduct that originated in Iran, its migration has occurred from the Middle East to Europe, China and India over the past 2000 years. (Fig. 03) This discovery supports the theory that Indigenous knowledge and infrastructure can migrate to similar biomes while adopting different materials and deployment. The ambition of this body of work is to document the design of these ancient innovations that have evolved in symbiosis with nature and are embedded, within nature, with a sensibility towards sustainability that's innate within the wisdom of the Fourth World.

This article only begins to scratch the surface of the culturally diverse, environmentally symbiotic and ecologically sound innovations that exist in the Fourth World. Such innovations are based upon wisdom that is flexible, adaptable and in line with the future of designing for climate resilience and a new model for conservation. The Fourth World's Indigenous infrastructures exist at the far reaches of the globe. The consequence of their loss will be far greater than we currently realise. Unraveling the complexities of ancient innovations will alter our engagement with the Fourth World, the natural world and, to a degree, determine humankind's potential for creative co-existence.

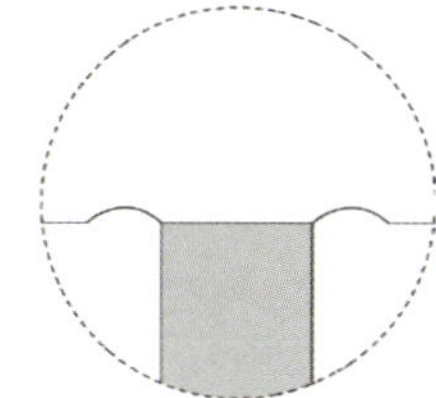

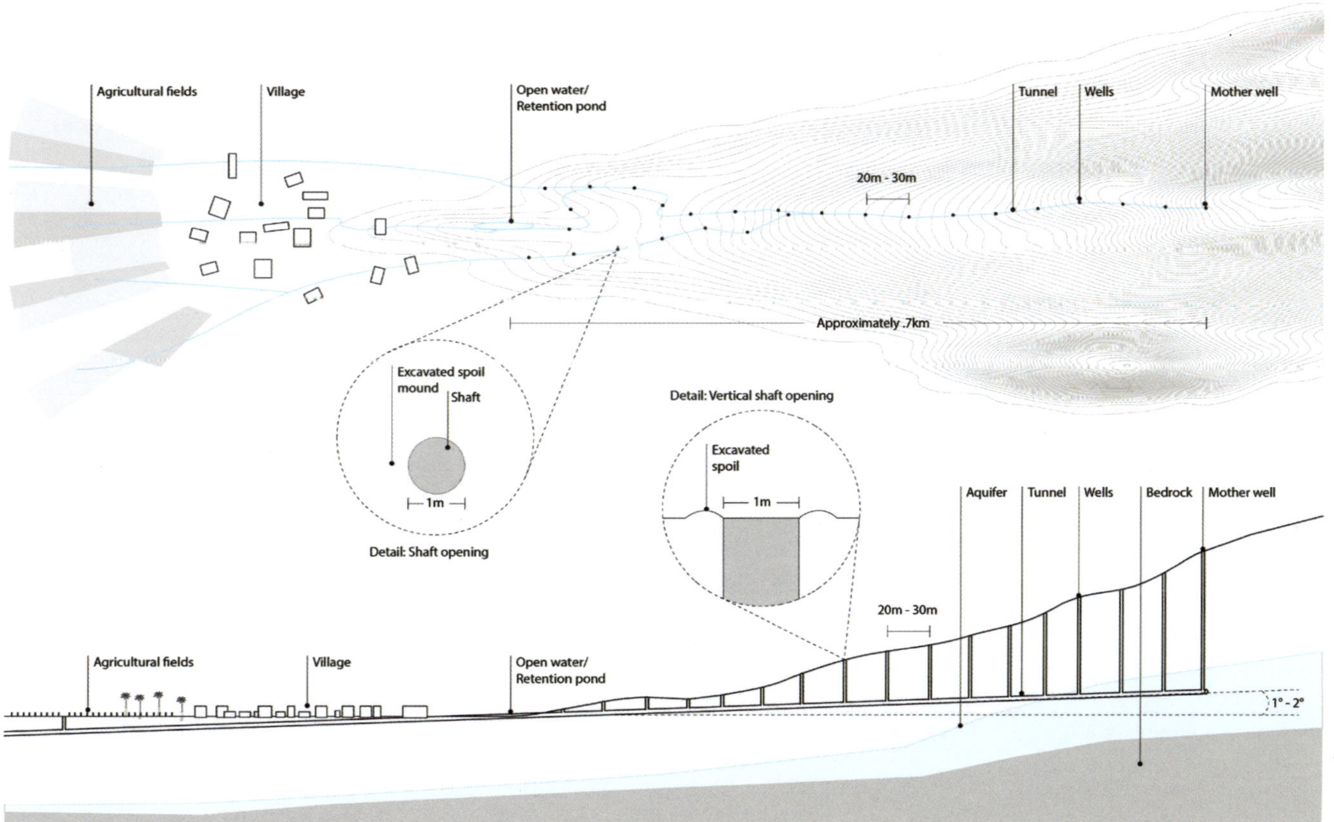

Figure 03. The *Qanat*: An underground aqueduct system origination in the Middle East and spreading globally over 2000 years.

"THE INDIAN QUESTION" AND THE POLITICAL DIFFUSION OF INDIAN RESERVATION POLICY FROM CANADA TO SOUTH AFRICA

Pierre Bélanger with Kate Yoon

The following is an excerpt from Canada's Apartheid: The Sanctioned Diffusion of Canadian Strategies of Indigenous Segregation, Assimilation, and Extermination in Extraction Empire: Undermining the Systems, States, and Scales of Canada's Global Resource Empire, 2017 - 1217, edited by Pierre Bélanger, published by MIT Press, Cambridge, MA in 2018.

In the Canadian government's Indian Affairs Central Registry Files (RG10, Volume 8588, 1/1-10-4), a file regarding liaison activities with the Union of South Africa concerning Native Affairs, shows that the Canadian government received reports from South Africa regarding the Department of Native Affairs, including one on the 'Resettlement of Natives'. In this file, there are also correspondences about visits of South African officials to Canada. One of the most high-profile visits is that by the South African Ambassador to Canada, W Dirkse van Schalkwyk, in 1962. According to formal government correspondence, 'His Excellency has expressed a deep interest in the Indian population and we have already assured him of our willingness to be of service and assistance should he wish to visit reserves...'[1]

In a follow-up letter to the Director of the Indian Affairs Branch, Department of Citizenship & Immigration, WPB Pugh, Superintendent of Stony/Sarcee Indian Agency, wrote:

> I drove [Dirkse van Schalkwyk] out to the Morley Indian Residential School where he toured the school with Mr. R.F. Campbell, principal, seeing the classrooms, dormitory, and general lay-out of the school. We only met one or two Indians for which I was disappointed. There was to have been a barbecue at the school at 3:00p.m., but in good old fashion Indian timing when we left at 4:00p.m., it was still not under way. On the return trip to Calgary, I drove him through the Sarcee Indian Reserve from one end to the other, showing him leases, community pasture and new homes, but time did not permit us to visit any of the homes.[2]

The Assistant Regional Supervisor of Manitoba wrote to Ottawa that:

> ... during the trip, His Excellency showed keen interest, and asked innumerable questions concerning the origins, status and customs of the Indian people on these Reserves; their form of band Government, and the social problems prevalent amongst them; and the relationship of our administration to them. I believe his questions were all answered adequately, and it was most interesting to hear his observations on the native people of South Africa and the seeming points of resemblance and dis-similarity between them and our people.[3]

Dirkse van Schalkwyk was reported as being 'most anxious to have a quick look at one of the Indian reserves in the Region', visiting Fort Alexander Reserve, Brokenhead Reserve, Duck Lake Agency, Beardy's Reserve, and the Ermineskin Reserve.[4] It is unclear where specifically Dirkse van Schalkwyk's interest in reserves stemmed from, but the year in which these events took place might give us a better understanding. 1962 was during the height of apartheid in South Africa. It was the year in which domestic and international protests escalated, and Nelson Mandela was arrested for conspiracy to overthrow the state. Amid this turmoil in South Africa was the ever-pressing political discussion of the "native question," and it seems that Canada suggested potential solutions in its light.

Furthermore, in a conversation on 16 February 2018, with former South African Ambassador to Canada (1985-1988), Glenn Babb iterated South Africa's

1. Indian Affairs Record Group 10, Library and Archives Canada, Vol. 8588, File 1/1-10-4 (1949–1962), MS, RG10 (Indian Afairs Central Registry Files) Ottawa, ON, 13 December 1956, viewed 14 September 2018.

2. Ibid 1.

3. Ibid 1.

4. Ibid 1.

5. For a discussion of the historical development of Indian reserves, see Bartlett, R 1990, Indian Reserves and Aboriginal Lands in Canada: A Homeland, Saskatoon, University of Saskatchewan.

6. See Steward, GA 1889, 'Report of the Superintendent of Rocky Mountains Park', 1 February 1888, Part VI in Canada Department of the Interior, 'Annual Report of the Department of the Interior for the Year 1887', Ottawa, ON, Queens Printer, p.10.

7. See Spence, MD 1999, Dispossessing the Wilderness: Indian Removal and the Making of the National Parks, New York, Oxford Unviersity Press, p. 4. On the deep-rooted entrenchment of this systemic axis, see Frank Tough's Research Note, 'Conservation and the Indian: Clifford Sifton's Commission of Conservation, 1910–1919,' Native Studies Review vol. 8, no. 2, 1992, pp. 61-77; and Robert Jago's incisive profile, 'Canada's National Parks are Colonial Crime Scenes: Many Canadians see wilderness as a right of citizenship. But the concept of Canada as a wilderness is unrecognizable to me and to other Indigenous people', The Walrus, viewed 30 June 2017, https://thewalrus.ca/canadas-national-parks-are-colonial-crime-scenes/.

8. See Savage, R 2013, 'Modern Genocidal Dehumanization: A New Model,' Patterns of Prejudice, vol. 47, no. 2, p. 159.

Timeline of Canadian Indian Reservations.
Image credit: OPSYS/ Landscape Infrastructure Lab/
Tiffany Kaewen Dang

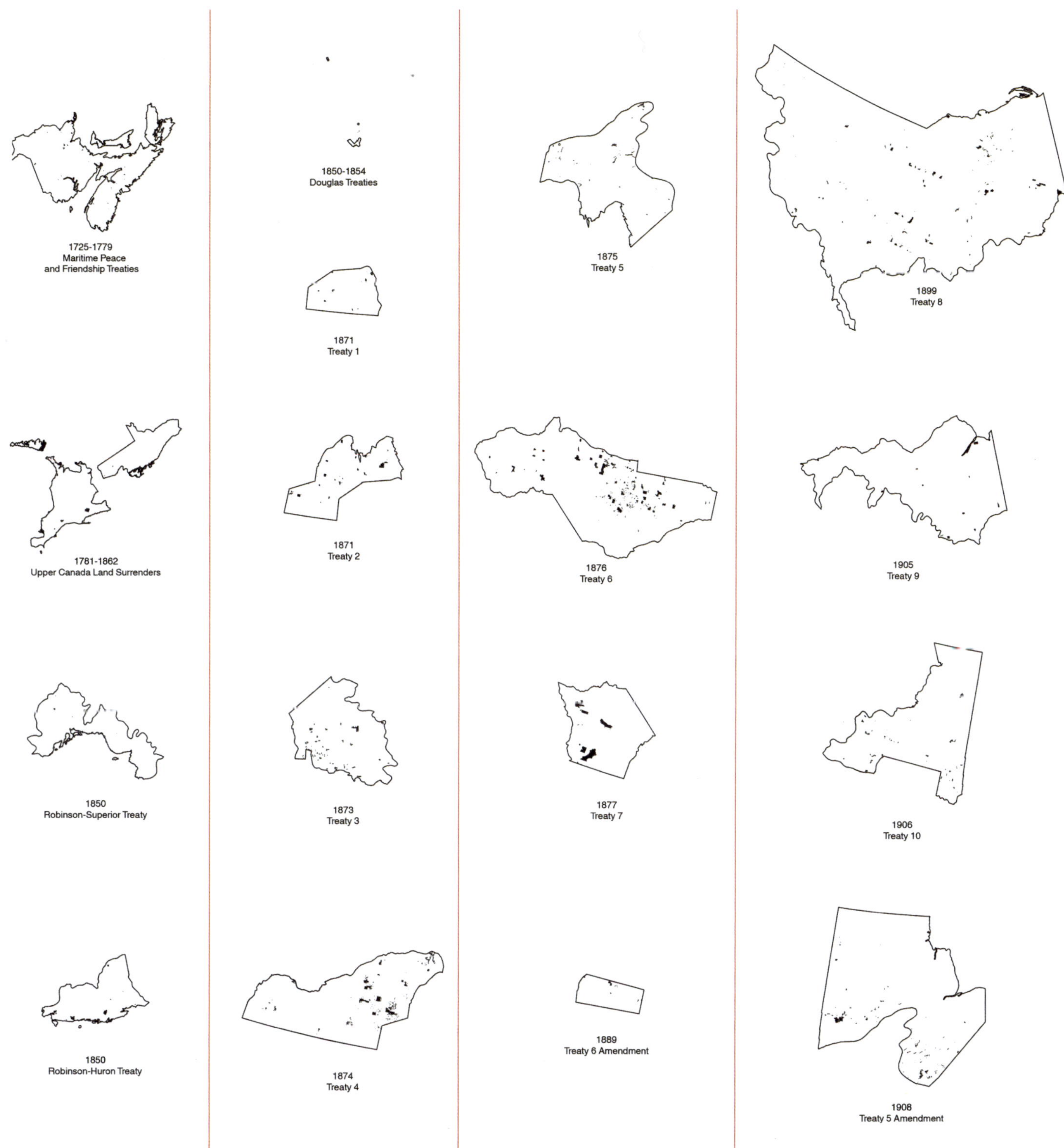

longstanding awareness of Canada's territorial segregation through Indian Reserves, ever since the inception of Canada's 1876 Indian Act and well into the mid-twentieth century. 'The Canadian Example' of Indian Reserves, as Babb referred to it, had been an important model for South Africa's creation of 'Homelands', the racially-based reserves proposed in the 1955 Tomlinson Report, especially with the growing native (black) population immigrating southward and moving in urban areas. Acknowledging that "Native Reserves" (Homelands) and the system of apartheid failed to secure what was essentially the control, livelihood, and security of the Afrikaners (whites), the administration of over 300 Indian Reserves in Canada across such a vast and remote area was of particular importance. In the context of growing urbanisation, the Canadian example was seen from the South African perspective as the assimilation of a rapidly growing, population of over 1 million Indigenous people living off-reserve, in Canadian cities and towns.[i]

The Canadian National Archives currently house a surprising abundance of information regarding liaison activities with other countries and the exchange of knowledge about the "native question." As John Leslie, historian of the Indian Act, said in a personal phone call on 6 July 2016, Resource Group 10 (Indian Affairs) is the biggest collection in Library and Archives Canada because the influence of Indians, then as is now, pervaded every sector of the economy and the culture of the country: 'for a marginalized peoples, they're everywhere'.

Finally, a fourth and perhaps more speculative understanding of the evolution of the treatment and administration of "Natives" emerges from the etymology and transfer of the word "reserves," "reservations," and "reserved lands" that originated, as noted in the Proclamation of 1763, under the mandate of reserving and setting aside lands exclusively for Natives in Canada by order of the King George III. The spatial process of reservation of land, and later that of "Natives," can be said to have evolved from the original process of reservation that applied to forests and other natural resources in earlier centuries. One of the most notable examples, and perhaps one of the more structural cases, is the utilisation of forest reserves, which emerged out of the ground-breaking Forest Charter of 1217, a component of the 1215 Magna Carta, which allocated civil rights and individual freedoms on territories that once belonged exclusively to the King and the Monarchy. The progression and evolution of the idea of reserving "forests," reserving "resources," reserving "land," or reserving "peoples,"[5] can also be said to be a natural progression of a spatially and legally enforceable technique used in monarchic and military regimes, easily transferred under the ideology of preservation and conservation to specially-designated peoples and native peoples of territories invaded and colonised thereafter, over the course of several centuries.

From Indian reservation to resource conservation, Canadian policies to control and contain Indigenous peoples through the creation of Indian Reserves from the early to mid-nineteenth century are inseparable from policies of Indian removal and exclusion in the creation of Canada's National Parks in the late nineteenth century. Established between 1885 and 1887 as the prototype for Canada's National Park System, the removal and exclusion of Indians in the Rocky Mountains Park (renamed Banff National Park after the passage of the National Parks Act in 1930) was a necessary part of, if not contingent on, these dual policies.

As the first Superintendent of Rocky Mountains Park George Stewart stated to the Minister of the Interior, Thomas White, on 1st February 1888 (following Rocky Mountains Park Act on 23 June 1887): 'It is of great importance that if possible the Indians should be excluded from the Park. Their destruction of the game and depredations among the ornamental trees make their too frequent visits to the Park a matter of great concern.'[6]

Furthermore, with westward land settlement across the prairies, the Treaty 7 of 1877 laid legislative groundwork prior to the creation of the Rocky Mountains Park in the early mid-1880s, for the creation of the three largest Indian reserves in Canada: Stoney 142-143-144, Blood 148, and Siksika 146. In order to maintain and enforce the exclusion of Indians and access to game in the wide expanse of the Rocky Mountains Park, 'the removal and exclusion of trespassers' was therefore an important clause (modelled on the Yellowstone Park Act of 1872) of the Rocky Mountains Park Act of 1887. Not uncoincidentally, the inception of the dual administration of Indian Affairs and nascent National Parks (under the banner of resource conservation and management) was made possible by the Department of Interior and the 1876 Indian Act, a consolidation of colonial Indian legislation by the first presiding Prime Minister of Canada, John A Macdonald. As historian Mark David Spence astutely observes 'the dual "island" system of nature preserves and Indian reservations' emerging in North America, including the examples of Yellowstone National Park in 1872 (US) and Rocky Mountains Park in 1887 (Canada), influenced a series of successive national parks and reserves in other British colonies, including the Royal National Park in 1879 (Australia), and Sabi Game Reserve in 1892 (South Africa) to name a few. Resource conservation and romanticisation of wilderness thus served as masks for Indian removal, exclusion, and erasure:

> The idealisation of uninhabited landscapes and the establishment of the first national parks also reflect important developments in late nineteenth century Indian policy. Much as the conquest of the West reshaped ideas about wilderness, it also led to the creation of an extensive reservation system. Ultimately, these isolated patches of land came to represent the final refuge of the [North] American Indian, and by the late 1860s and early 1870s, [settlers] regarded reservations, rather than 'wilderness,' as the appropriate place for all Indians to live.[7]

In Canada today, strategies of territorial dispossession that span Indian Reserves and National Parks lie along a tight, integrated axis of resource conservation and racial segregation, which is continuous and relatively unchallenged. In effect, the process of displacing and concentrating Indigenous peoples, whether "Indians" in Canada or "Natives" in South Africa, was essentially commensurate with a process of dehumanisation.[8]

i. Conversation by authors with Glenn Babb, 16 February 2017. To elaborate on the different forms of segregation that interested South Africa during Apartheid, sociologist and anthropologist from the Belgian Congo, Pierre Van Den Berghe observed in the late 1960s that Homelands were being conceived as variations of territorial and urban segregation:

> [m]eso-segregation is considerably costlier but on it rests the political control of the highly explosive urban areas. From the viewpoint of the maintenance of White supremacy meso-segregation is thus essential. Only through the compartmentalization of racial groups into streamlined ghettoes can the dominant White minority hope to combat open insurgency. On the other hand the implementation of meso-segregation with the entire repressive machinery of reference books influx control job reservation population registration and group areas is directly responsible for the overwhelming majority of acts of protest and revolt against apartheid. Thus the ghettoization of urban life brings with it the growing hypertrophy of the police and military apparatus. Not only is the militarization of an ever-growing proportion of the White population expensive but its effectiveness is limited by at least two factors. First the open and unrestrained use of military violence given the climate of world opinion threatens the government with outside intervention. Second as the Whites monopolize all key positions in government industry transport communications etc. and as many Whites hold such key positions the simultaneous mobilization of the albinocracy on any sizeable scale would bring about considerable disruption of civilian activities not to mention the problem of the protection of dependents."

Van Den Berghe, PL 1996, 'Racial Segregation in South Africa: Degrees and Kinds,' Cahiers d'Études Africaines, vol. 6, no. 23, pp 418.

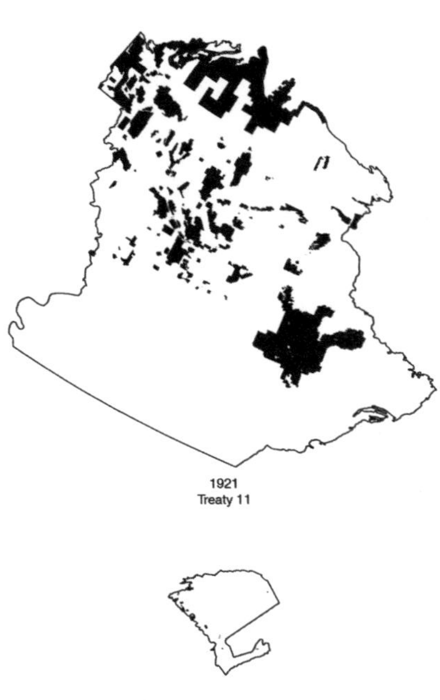

1921
Treaty 11

1923
Williams Treaties

1993
Nunavut Land Claims Agreement

EAT THE STREET

Juliette Anich

What better way to get to know the place you find yourself than walking? One foot in front of another as many explorers had done before me, I sought to understand the spaces and character of this place I found myself in. Outside of the comforts of the private realm, outside in the elements. Feeling the terrain of the pavement under foot, the heat of the midday sun and the neighbours cats who patrol the streets, I slowly begin to uncover the narrative of the space. It is not until the space is walked that smaller details can be appreciated. The handwritten note on the front gate asking for the postal man to come around the back due to a baby sleeping; the noisy dog who spooks easily behind a high fence; the broken tiles on the side of the old pub and the new paint job of neighbours fence. These details record the daily lives of a place putting meaning and purpose into a space.

I had gotten to know my way around my suburb so I could navigate the fastest way between points A and B, but now I found myself exploring the most 'interesting' way from points A to B. What drew my interest as I explored the place around me was where the natural world was blossoming in the most unlikely places, in the middle of a city on curb sides, between fences, and on forgotten pockets of land.

Bradley L. Garret is an urban explorer who explores places such as sites marked for demolition, sites under construction, or those shut off from public access. He describes urban exploration as 'a search for experiences located at the porous, live intersections between bodies and places in (re) discovered locations'.[1]

I began to find I was generating meaning from the spaces between nature and culture, and I was particularly interested in where this boundary blurs. Inspired by an artist collective in Los Angeles (LA) called Fallen Fruit, I decided to document where food was being grown on and over public land in Cooks Hill, to create a public fruit map.[2]

As I walked and mapped the more I realised that I was joining in a tradition of explorers documenting newfound places, walking quite literally in their footsteps. Unexpectedly for me, I found that I was documenting and celebrating a feature that modern cartography had chosen to omit, being replaced with the markings of major shopping centres and other venues that score highly on search engine analytics. But at the same time, food growing in a place offers unquestionable insights into the way of life in times past.[3]

The inner city suburb streets that I was walking echoed the post war life in Australia that was characterised by southern European immigration. Despite the availability and affordability of fresh produce available to buy in Australia at this time, many migrants wanted to continue their own traditions of growing food, and importantly their own types of food which were not commercially available. Migrants planted and grew olives, grape vines, plums, apples, pears, lemons, figs and apricot trees. Cultivating their place, with the food they wanted to grow was an act of settlement and the beginning to make space to belong.[4]

I found that the boundaries of a place were as liberating as they were binary. I liked that I only had so much of a place to map, otherwise I could be going forever! So I embraced the suburban boundary, developing a slow and evolving understanding that feeling free requires embracing constraints.

Nature though, seems to respect no constraints, seeing only barriers that need to be overcome in the never-ending task to find water, sun and space. The natural quirks in cartography interested me as they would not be boxed in and would not respect an arbitrary line on a piece of paper. During my walks I discovered more and more fruit trees and plants that crossed over from private to public land; I was curious about where the boundary of trespassing stood. Was there an imaginary line where the border of the private property was marked, so anything over public land; was available for all? But what if I could stand on public land and still reach the fruit. Was this fair game? Fallen Fruit in LA held a campaign titled 'Plant the Perimeter', encouraging residents to plant fruit trees along the perimeter of their land to encourage sharing and neighbourly interaction. Fallen Fruit was proposing that fruit growing along the fence line could be the proverbial olive branch between urban foragers (those people who eat what they come across without cultivating anything themselves) and urban growers. However, the philosopher, Henri Lefebvre, suggests that 'the organization of space is never neutral, but always entangled in complex power arrangements'.[5]

Sharing the map with others was always my intention for the project. Once I finished my suburb, I transferred the information from a hand drawn map into a digital version. I created a blog, explored social media and connected with others who, just like me, were all mapping food that was growing on or over public land in the areas local to them all around the world. Discovering and connecting with other mappers across Australia and internationally was embracing and supportive – a community of like minded groups and individuals who were united by their endeavours to support local food production, connecting with the local environment and celebrating shared ownership. Shortly after this connection and embrace with other mappers, it was collectively decided that a larger, more comprehensive mapping platform be developed which would combine all the sites. This would enable the continuation of mapping should one group dissolve or attention of one person move on.

The project was picked up by a journalist from Sydney writing about the local food movement. An article, profiling the project and other local food community centric projects, appeared in the Sun Herald in October 2010 on a Sunday.[6] It included a photograph of me in a community garden on public land and a section of the online map featuring locations of where food is grown on, or over public land, across three lower north shore suburbs in Sydney.

This article and the mapping project outraged many. Most of the people that came forward with complaints were members of a community garden where I was photographed for the article. I wasn't living in Sydney at the time of the media release but family members were. Using the White Pages, members from the community garden personally visited the house of those

1. Garrett, BL 2013, Explore Everything: Place-Hacking the City, London, Verso.

2. Fallen Fruit, 2010, Los Angeles, viewed 5 March 2015, http://fallenfruit.org/

3. Harzinski, K 2010, From Here To There: A Curious Collection from the Hand Drawn Map Association, New York, Princeton Architectural Press.

4. Gaynor, A 2006, Harvest of the Suburbs: An environmental history of growing food in Australian Cities, Crawley, University of Western Australia Press.

5. De Certau, M 1984, The Practice of Everyday Life, Berkeley, University of California Press.

6. Wood, A 2010, Fresh Food Takes Root In Cities, Sun Herald, 21 November, viewed 21 November 2010, http://www.smh.com.au/lifestyle/diet-and-fitness/fresh-food-takes-root-in-cities-20101120-181uf.html?skin=text-only

relatives living in Sydney to confront the author (apparently, me!) about the actions. I missed being confronted with pitchforks at dawn and, in lieu, a conversation ensued over email and through comments left on the blog. The members of the community garden felt that by sharing the locations of where food is grown on or over public land, I was taking advantage of their hard work in developing the garden and was promoting the idea of taking without contributing. Their arguments were highly emotive and demonstrate the deep passions stirred by my transgression. Here are a few of my favourite (read: ego squashing) quotes: 'Your information is likely to spell the end of the Community Garden, a garden that was built from the ground up with our bare hands. Volunteers are highly unlikely to continue a commitment if the fruits of their labours are stolen from them.' 'Why should I continue to donate my TIME and MONEY for people like yourself to reap all of the benefits.' Or the following three:

> The line 'It tastes so much better, and if you pick respectfully, community gardening can alleviate pressure on our food systems.' This last line, especially with respect to the fact that the MPCG is in fact labelled a 'Community Garden,' is particularly distressing for all of us involved. Moreover, the proof is in the pudding, in that numerous people (some with article in hand) came down on Sunday to see what food was on offer for them to pick and take home.
>
> Whilst we can't, and never intend to, control who enters the garden, up until this point we have never had a problem with people taking stuff from the garden.
>
> It is a very thin veil that you cloak yourself in with regards to your statement that if "the map not be used in the way it was intended then unfortunately it is out of my control." Similarly to all of those businesses (think Napster and other file and torrent sharing sites) that are currently being prosecuted for enabling illegal behaviour, you too have a responsibility (if you believe it only to be a moral one) to ensure that the information that you publish is accurate and do everything you can to reduce the risk it will be misunderstood and used for unintended purposes.

What had started as a personal project of interest grew, in what felt like overnight, into a broader study of perceived land ownership and rights, community engagement and perceptions of waste in a developed urban landscape. It occurred to me that these gardeners of the commons, of land given by their local council, to the community, was being protected as if a private retreat of an exclusive club, an extension of their own backyards.

The transition of the project between private and public was facilitated by online creative commons licensing and mainstream media coverage. The transition was smooth in likeminded circles but turbulent beyond. The support of other mappers across Australia and internationally contradicted starkly with the backlash of a small gardening group. I found that the same motivations uniting the group of mappers were the same as those that divided the broader community. Groups involved in community gardens, and individuals who openly cultivated land outside their private land holdings, were particularly perturbed by the idea of sharing not only the locations of their cultivated sites, but also the produce. They felt that as the ones putting the effort into growing, they should not have to share with others. Their actions, although motivated by broader global issues such as climate change, fossil fuel depletion and food security, were put into practice to protect themselves, not others. The self-interest motivator, often cited as a positive agent of change in green purchases and involvement in the sustainability movement was, in this instance, used as a tool to identify and segregate socially. Counter to trends around sharing, and discourse around the unifying nature of community food production, the backlash was evidence of a discord between sustainability intentions and selflessness. The experience begged the question: which was more important, a society growing food for themselves? Or a society willing to share food grown together?

AT LAKE MUNGO

Louis Mitchell

Lake Mungo is a dry lake located in the World Heritage protected Willandra region of New South Wales, Australia. Home to the Barkindj, Nyiampaa and Mutthi Mutthi people. Humans have inhabited this area for as long as 50,000 years. It is the resting place of Mungo Man and Mungo Woman, the oldest Aboriginal remains found in Australia, dating back to more than 40,000 years old.

THINKING IN COUNTRY

Darcy Rankin

In considering Country I recognise that I approach it as both a settler and outsider-inside. I also acknowledge that my existence as a settler is enabled by the Country in which I live and work and that I am enveloped by this Country. I am not initiated and lack the cultural permissions and knowledges to articulate the depth and intricacy of relationship that specific 'Country' embodies. In considering Country as an outsider, I engage it partially as a concept. This is problematic as a mode of approach that implies both a knowability and a distance which I am not afforded. This tension will be addressed critically within the essay along with crucial issues concerning 'cultural' appropriation and environmental management.

The opportunity to engage with Country is a generous gift from Indigenous 'Australia', which is continuously offered even in the midst of ongoing colonial adversity that threatens the very hands that hold out this gift. Country then is strong, dynamic, and robust enough to offer an understanding and appeal against the Western structures of thought that propagate colonial violence and socio-ecological degradation. In this way, Country fundamentally de-centres the Western paradigm while simultaneously and continuously enunciating alternative Indigenous realities. This essay will explore the particular implications of Country for 'environmental' management in the 'Australian' context.

WESTERN METAPHYSICS

Before Country can be understood at the depth required here, we must articulate the Western conceptual base with which it contrasts. Country is not merely an element of an opposing Indigenous ontology, one that is merely differing. Instead, Country embodies an opposition to ontology itself as a category particular to the metaphysical tradition of the West. Discourses framing Indigenous world-views as ontologies then could be understood as attempts to subsume Indigeneity into a "larger" Western metaphysical taxonomic program of ontology. This is particularly problematic where metaphysics as a particular frame of thought can be foundationally derived from the Institutions of imperialism, colonialism, industrialisation and capitalism, variously responsible for the production of the anthropocene.[1]

Metaphysics is a particular and contingent Western conceptual project that some theorists have located as stemming from the advent of particular modes of agricultural practice.[2] Metaphysics is not then a super-organic framework for contextualizing different ontologies within and alongside the Western ontology, the study of being, is a Western metaphysical concern that can be problematised within the heritage of dualism as necessarily implying an external category of that which is not being, non-being, as an outside, a domain which may be exploited, colonised or polluted.

By constructing a category for "being" as rational agents with minds in the cartesian tradition, we simultaneously produce a distinction for that which isn't being as non-rational.[3] Philosophy as metaphysically instituted then, has always had a 'view about nature'.[4] It produces this exterior domain necessarily. In platonic thought, for instance, the metaphysical concern for Ideal Forms, inversely produces a domain of non-being, the worldly domain that is not-contingent, extrinsic to being, and corrupted.[5] 'Nature' then, as a domain, is a recent and highly contingent conceptual production of the metaphysical concern itself, and not a universally understood category.[6] Metaphysics is then the foundation for Western hierarchies and problematic categorical dualisms. [7,8]

The concern for being produces a differential categorization and the external 'not-being' is rendered as extrinsic or outside. But as being is permeated by non-being, these categories have to be constantly re-articulated to retain differential meaning, resulting in an ongoing violence of exclusion. Inversely, through the violence of inclusion, this system could be seen as structurally enabling the inherent violence of mass domestication.[9]

As such, this metaphysical difference is systematically deferred to some future posited point of separation. For example, in the platonic concern toward death, this metaphysical difference would be realised and the spirit would move finally into the world of Ideal Forms.[10] The possibility of being is maintained through orientation toward some future point of realised transcendence. This is epitomised in Elon Musk's Mars One project, wherein terrestrial transcendence of Earth's ecological conditions would constitute a kind of teleological realisation of humanity, a separation, and realisation of "nature" as an actual discrete domain.

This process of categorical differentiation is also embedded in language. Since the Roman institution of private property, self as the 'I' that owns property comes into existence negatively through this assertion of ownership.[11]

In the settler colonial encounter with Indigenous Sovereignty, this 'I' is produced negatively through the structural marginalisation of newer migrants. The national 'Australian' 'I' as in the 'this is mine' proclamation, is inferred negatively through an unendingly violent announcement to newer-comers, 'this is not yours'.[12]

COUNTRY

Country is well described by Deborah Bird Rose in Nourishing Terrains as "multi-dimensional" and "consisting of people, animals, plants, Dreamings; underground, earth, soils, minerals and waters, surface water, and air."[13]

Rose expands:

> People say that Country knows, hears, smells, takes notice, takes care, is sorry or happy. Country is not a generalised or undifferentiated type of place, such as one might indicate with terms like 'spending a day in the country' or 'going up the country'. Rather, Country is a living entity with a yesterday, today and tomorrow, with a consciousness, and a will toward life. Because of this richness, Country is home, and peace; nourishment for body, mind, and spirit; heart's ease.[14]

Unlike in the Western tradition, Country does not refer to a categorically exclusive domain like 'Nature' or 'Environment', and so, neither enables or requires a differential category of self as in the Western metaphysical tradition. Country exceeds metaphysics in referring to an unfolding process of which one is part, but through which things cannot be totalised.

Differing from the Western metaphysical categorization of being (self) and non being (nature), Country doesn't generate an arbitrary fenced boundary between the sentient categorizer and external category, 'Country is also sentient, communicative, relational and interactive'.[15]

In this way the evaluative onus is not on the 'environmentally' encompassed subject. Instead, management decisions are informed by a dialogue with Country encompassing spirits, landscape features, places, plants, and animals. This is articulated in Dreamings passed through Country, learned, and by listening and talking to Country.[16]

> People say that Country is aware, it knows what's going on, it knows who's there, and It knows if they have a right to be there. Other animals also watch, laugh at our mistakes, and take notice of our better actions. So too do all the people who have passed away who are still there in their own Country, taking care of it.[17]

The Dreamings of Country are told by Country and are passed on through Country. This process continually ties people to place, in a process of mutual becoming. Self is grown up relationally within Country[18] following behind the ancestors.[19] This is different to the Western system of selfhood which is generated via exclusion and distinction from a projected exclusive domain. One cares for self as they care for Country, as these are not exclusive categories. There is then what could be understood as an intrinsic ethical relationship embodied in Country. There is less difference between acting on behalf of oneself and on behalf of Country, especially in the long term.[7] The value based judgements of Ethical problems don't necessarily 'fit easily into an Aboriginal world-view.'[20]

One illustration of this is that, for Indigenous Peoples, Country that has been cared for and lived in is considered healthy and quiet, whereas Country without this entwined relationship is considered wild.[21] This directly contrasts with the contention in the Western nature-culture duality wherein human presence in nature is corruption, while the untouched 'wilderness' is pristine.[22]

The encompassing field outside Country is guaranteed in its incapacity to be totalised, outside this Country there is another Country, and so on, everything is situated relationally.[23] In this way Country is radically dynamic, and new occurrences actually validate this non-totalisable quality of Country, new things belong necessarily, and soon assume situated relational meaning.[24] The metaphysical world view attempting to generate Colonial 'Australia' in this sense is subsumed within Country. The *Gardiya* (whitefellas) are subsumed and situated within Country even while wandering around asserting their self through differential property logics such

1. Morton, T 2016 Dark Ecology For a Future of Coexistence, New York, Columbia University Press.

2. Ibid 1.

3. Plumwood, V 1990, Plato and the Bush: Philosophy and the environment in Australia, Meanjin, vol 49, no 3, pp 524-536.

4. Ibid 3.

5. Ibid 3.

6. Descola, P, Lloyd, J & Sahlins, M 2005, Beyond nature and culture, Chicago, University of Chicago Press.

7. Mathews, F 1995, Community and the Ecological Self, Environmental Politics, vol 4, no 4, pp 66-100.

8. Mathews, F 2004, Land Metaphysics Dialogue, viewed 2 June 2015, http://www.freyamathews.net/downloads/LandMetaphysics.pdf

9. Ibid 1.

10. Ibid 3.

11. Niccolacopoulos, T & Vassilacopoulos, G 2014, Indigenous Sovereignty and the The Being of the Occupier; Manifesto For a White Philosophy of Origins, Re-press.

12. Ibid 11.

13. Rose, D 1996 Nourishing Terrains, Canberra, Australian Heritage Commission.

14. Ibid 13.

15. Rose, D 2013, Val Plumwood's Philosophical Animism: attentive interactions in the sentient world, Environmental Humanities, vol 3, pp 93-109.

16. Ibid 13.

17. Ibid 13.

18. Ibid 13.

19. Rose, D 2004, Reports From a Wild Country Ethics For Decolonisation, UNSW Press.

20. Ibid 13.

21. Rose, D 1998, Exploring an Aboriginal Land Ethic, Meanjin, vol 47, no 3, pp 3-387.
22. Ibid 21.

23. Ibid 15.

24. Ibid 13.

25. Ibid 13

as is illustrated in this quote from Anzac Munnganyi: "White people just came up blind, bumping into everything. And put the flag; put the flag."[25]

Another example of the radical non-totalising openness of Country is given by Bruce Pascoe in Dark Emu, where he recounts from Charles Sturt's journals how, near Cooper's Creek, Sturt's exhausted party encountered a large group of Aboriginal people. Sturt quoted in Pascoe:

> Had these people been of an unfriendly temper, we could not in any possibility have escaped them, for our horses could not have broken into a canter to save our lives or their own. We were therefore wholly in their power ... but, so far from exhibiting any unkind feeling, they treated us with genuine hospitality, and we might certainly have commanded whatever they had. Several of them brought us large troughs of water, and when we had taken a little, held them up for our horses to drink; an instance of nerve that is very remarkable, for I am quite sure that no white man (having never seen or heard of a horse before, and with the natural apprehension the first sight of such an animal would create) would deliberately have walked up to what must have appeared to them most formidable brutes, and placing the troughs they carried against their breast, they allowed the horses to drink, with their noses almost touching them. They likewise offered us some roasted ducks, and some cake. When we walked over to their camp, they pointed to a large new hut, and told us we could sleep there ... and (later) they brought a quantity of sticks for us to make a fire, wood being extremely scarce.[26]

Whereas in the Western metaphysics of exclusion such an event would surely generate an initial hostility toward the 'alien' outsiders, in this instance the radical openness of Country as non-totalisisable and non-excluding enables relational empathy as a primary inclusive response. In this way Country can be understood as regenerative, dynamic, adaptive and open. This quality directly problematises discourses concerning a 'cultural' authenticity of Indigenous peoples, which is projected onto them by the demands of institutions like Native Title. 'cultural' discontinuity actually arises as a function of inflexible Western systems of thought, which, premised on exclusion and difference, are closed and rigid.

'ENVIRONMENTAL' MANAGEMENT

Country then presents a fundamental critique of the Western metaphysical world-view. In this sense, Caring for Country would be inadequately equated to the Western ideas of 'environmental' management. This mistake is especially important considering that governmental programs of 'environmental' management usually consider Indigenous 'cultural' values as a mere component of their assessment.

Consider the phrase: 'The environment that "We" are in.' The 'We' as narrator is the witness of a separate Environmental category, simultaneously producing a differentiated category of self. The self as We comes into being differentially, it is extrinsic and so may implicitly function in spite of or against that 'environment', as anything not We. 'Environment' then as extrinsic from self, provides the possibility space for capitalist processes of extraction and pollution to occur by only providing an indirect contingency, and even despite our better judgement and benevolent intentions.
The 'environment' is also a metaphysical totality that can be considered problematic in the same way as nature in that its normativity demands a continuous repetition of violence of exclusion.[27] In this way it is intimately related to the linear procedure of time.[28]

As such there are fundamental problems in enunciating it in terms of management. The use of 'environment' in terms of management negatively generates this separated categorical 'self'. This differentiated self must then establish an ethical device in order to reconcile its interests with the extent of that 'environment', to negotiate the distance implied by the fence as such. environmentalism arises to pursue these ends but through the structure of the terms it employs serves instead to reproduce violence.[29]

26. Pascoe, B 2014, Dark Emu, Broome, Magabala Books.

27. Morton, T 2009, Ecology Without Nature, Rethinking Environmental Aesthetics, Cambridge, Massachusetts, Harvard University Press.

28. Morton, T 2012, Ecology without the Present, Oxford Literary Review 34(2) pp 229-238.

29. Ibid 27.

30. Ibid 3.

31. Mitchell, D 1995, There's No Such Thing as Culture: Towards a Reconceptualization of the Idea of Culture in Geography, Transactions of the Institute of British Geographers, vol 20, no 1, pp 102.

32. Yunkaporta, T 2019, Online: https://www.linkedin.com/posts/tyson-yunkaporta-04a9b969_art-is-an-economic-weapon-of-war-when-it-activity-6561730120837672961-HCb6] Viewed 12/08/2019

The ethical project as directed towards the 'environment' is a demanding field for Western philosophy.[30] It is problematic as a project attempting to establish a norm, or uncover an inherent contingency between two metaphysical categories that are reliant on their difference. In attempting to reconcile ourselves with the environment we generally utilize the institution of objective knowledge. This process is often problematically retrospective, as the observational method requires effects in the first instance to observe a proven contingency, thereby implying a default non-contingency that must be disproved objectively. Action on global heating is deferred by this onus on objective evidence of proof that humans are even responsible. Within this system our understanding and management of an 'environment' requires degradation in the first instance, as it is premised on categorical exclusion.

An example of this is the concept of ecological services. They are ecological functions that can be objectively shown as existentially necessary to 'Us' as humans. The concept inversely implies that only certain ecological functions are necessary. While we are implored to act in particular instances according to this value for our discrete selves, the categorical distinction is simultaneously reinforced.

INDIGENOUS 'CULTURAL' VALUES OF THE 'ENVIRONMENT'

Considering the 'environment' in this way, as a fundamentally problematic Western metaphysical construction, we can accordingly see the colonialism inherent in the Australian context of 'environmental' management in regards to Indigenous interests and agendas.

The 'environment' isn't a concept necessarily shared in Indigenous world-views, and it isn't equatable with Country. Therefore, in supposedly addressing Indigenous concerns within a 'larger' framework of environmental management we are propagating yet another project of assimilation. Instead, we should be deferring to the ecological expertise of Indigenous stewardship of Sovereign Country over millennia.

The concept of 'culture', as a discrete category and the other half of the nature/culture dualism is just as problematic. The concern for Indigenous 'cultures' then is premised on a Western dualism in which 'culture' itself is a discrete category in opposition to 'nature'.

Like nature, culture is an idea that integrates by dividing.[31] By compartmentalising aspects of life as culture we imply that only some aspects of life are meaningful and so generate elsewhere a nihilistic plane for capitalist extraction, transaction and pollution to occur on. This plane is then subsequently populated with small - often elite - institutional ghettos of cultural production, which are then continuously further marginalised through the categorical demands of this exclusion. The arts then in this sense act as a vehicle for meaning to be removed from society at large. Consider this example from Tyson Yunkaporta:

> Art is an economic weapon of war when it is named 'art' and separated from life. Art mines the margins because that's where the value is. As minority artists we think ourselves radicals talking truth to power, but we are in fact the shock troops of gentrification, social fragmentation and our own ongoing dispossession. Collective imagination, not labour, is the only source of value - the arts industry co-opts that power. We perform our unique individual connection to land and community while destroying the collective knowledge of these things. I say to hell with art. We need to reabsorb this previously nameless process into our lives and reclaim our status as humans, as the custodians of creation.[32]

Country is not like the practice of environmental management as engaged via distanced hierarchical evaluation. Rather, Country exceeds and subsumes this framework. When utilizing an 'environmental' framework to address Indigenous Country we attempt to project onto it a problematic Western metaphysical scheme, and in doing so, enact further colonial violence.

In addressing Indigenous perspectives as 'cultural' values in the 'landscape' within a program of 'environmental' management, we simultaneously act to elevate the Western metaphysical system as a universal while attempting to limit and subsume Indigeneity into a settler metaphysical paradigm, again performing a further colonial violence under the guise of inclusion.

In engaging 'environmental' issues 'Australia' needs to reconsider how its metaphysical foundations and frames of reference, particularly those embodied in our governing structures, unwittingly propagate the socio-ecological problems they seek to address. Do National Parks provision for the protection of the 'nature' within or do they provision for the larger ongoing capitalist exploitation of land without?

CONCLUSION

By engaging Country while reflectively focusing on re-framing settler world-views in terms of their deficits as structurally implicated in colonial socio-ecological degradation, locally and globally we afford opportunities to reverse a colonial power dynamic and reorient ourselves to the success and authority of Indigenous peoples in stewarding Country over many millennia. In our circumstances of global capitalist ecological degradation, extinction, and global heating, this gift which Country offers us for reflection, reparation and diversion is paramount.

WRITING PLACES

Louise Chiodo

Talking about place, where we belong, is a constant subject for many of us. We want to know if it is possible to live on earth peacefully? Is it possible to sustain life? Can we embrace an ethos of sustainability that is not solely about the appropriate care of the world's resources but also about the creation of meaning – the making of lives that we feel are worth living? [1]

Belonging, exclusion, fragmented communities, displacement and debates about Indigenous peoples' rights to land are a global phenomenon, but they have a very particular relevance here in Australia. Land and landscape are inextricably linked to our cultural identities, politically, personally and historically. We are a land of migrants recent and old, and Indigenous Peoples. We are all grappling with a fraught history centred around land.

What does this mean for designers of the built environment? These issues are of importance to us because the tensions and power dynamics they produce are embedded in the spaces we come to design. They can also be reproduced through the act of design, regardless of our intention or awareness of issues of colonisation and dispossession on a conscious level. The Portrait Building, an apartment building directly behind the RMIT Design Hub, which features a huge portrait of Indigenous activist William Barak on its facade, is perhaps a case in point. It generated much controversy on its unveiling due to its problematic, or at least limited, honouring of Indigenous histories in Victoria relying heavily on visual reference over cultural values and connections.

The Parliamentary Triangle in Canberra provides another example. Though a typological understanding of the Parliamentary Triangle may place it more firmly in the category of national space and architecture criticism, we can ask how similar power dynamics and tensions manifest spatially in the design of more contemporary and everyday spaces. It also has a pertinency to landscape architecture in Australia. Parliament House was the most expensive architectural project Australia had seen at the time of its construction in 1988, and the first to foreground the role and expertise of the landscape architect. Literally inserted into the landscape to express the inextricable link between land and Australian cultural identity, this project highlighted the potential for landscape architects to lead large-scale projects at the front end as opposed to the usual practice at the time of coming in at the end after the architects' vision was finalised. Not two kilometres from Parliament House, on the same axis cutting through the Parliamentary Triangle, is the Aboriginal Tent Embassy,[2] a significant site and symbol of pan-Aboriginality, the land rights movement and Indigenous activism since 1972. The relationship between the Embassy and Parliament House speaks directly to these questions of identity in Australia, of belonging, displacement and unresolved issues of Indigenous sovereignties. While much has been written to celebrate the subversive power and important symbolism of the Tent Embassy, questions it raises about non-Indigenous identities in Australia are less often engaged with, at least in a design context.

1. Hooks, B 2008, Belonging: A Culture of Place, Taylor and Francis, New York.

2. Schaap, A, Foley, G & Howell, E, 2014. The Aboriginal Tent Embassy: Sovereignty, Black Power, Land Rights and the State, Routledge, Abingdon, Oxfordshire & New York.

3. Gammage, B 2012, The Biggest Estate on Earth: How Aborigines made Australia, Allen & Unwin, Crows Nest, NSW.

4. Pascoe, B 2014, Dark Emu: Black Seeds: Agriculture or Accident?, Magabala Books, Broome, Western Australia.

5. Rendell, J 2010, Site Writing: the Architecture of Art Criticism, I. B. Tauris, London, UK.

6. Grillner, K 2012, 'A Performative Mode of Writing Place: Out and About the Rosenlund Park, Stockholm, 2008–2010' in Stead, N 2012, Semi-Detached: Writing, Representation and Criticism in Architecture, Uro Publications, Melbourne, Australia.

There has been significant progress affecting landscape architects in Victoria with regards to engaging with Indigenous histories and ongoing connections to land. Together, a number of law and policy changes, institutional Reconciliation Action Plans (RAP), and other developments point to a shift with substantial implications for us in terms of both theory and practice. Legislative changes include the Aboriginal Heritage Act 2006, put in place to provide improved protection and management for Indigenous cultural heritage, including specific places, objects and intangible expressions of Indigenous cultural connections. Joined by the Aboriginal Heritage Regulations 2007, the 2006 Act was amended in 2016, and is currently undergoing further amendments to clarify the land forms that call for a cultural heritage management plan.

Indigenous Architecture and Design Victoria, known by its acronym IADV, emerged in 2010, with the goal of encouraging Indigenous communities to engage with the design of the built environment, and encouraging designers of the built environment to be more engaged with Indigenous culture. Founded by Melbourne-based Indigenous architects, Rueben Berg and Jefa Greenaway, the not-for-profit organisation emerged in response to the Australian Institute of Architects' (AIA) implementation of a RAP in the same year, which aimed to ensure appropriate Indigenous support and guidance is available to architects and designers attending to RAPs and related issues. Key education institutions for landscape architecture in Melbourne have recently implemented RAPs also. At the time of writing, the Victorian Chapter of the Australian Institute of Landscape Architects is about to launch its RAP. Though the process began a couple of years ago it is comparatively slow to action given our primary focus is land. Shifts in thinking have occurred regardless.

Recently published texts reflect and encourage a new understanding of land, disrupting conventional conceptions held by landscape architects and the wider community. Bill Gammage's The Biggest Estate on Earth,[3] and Bruce Pascoe's Dark Emu[4] are two of the most significant of these texts. Interestingly, both draw on colonial representations and descriptions to disrupt older conceptions of land. Based on Gammage's interpretation of early colonial writings and art work documenting Australian landscapes, his work shows Indigenous land management practices were far more systematic and scientific than has been previously acknowledged. Pascoe shines further light on the existence of Indigenous land management practices, including extensive food technologies. His findings are also informed by the writings of early explorers, histories that have been omitted or at least largely downplayed from dominant narratives of Australia's past.

The students of landscape architecture who I work with have an interest in Indigenous histories and ongoing connections to land that is far more pervasive than when I was a student a decade ago. However, I find it difficult to point directly to examples where designers have applied the appropriate tools and frameworks for meaningful and reflexive engagement. As designers, we often take a problem-solving approach to our work, usually under pressure to produce a design outcome within a limited timeframe and negotiating many other restraints and requirements of a given design brief. In an education and research context our designs and interventions are often conceptualised as "testing" but we research through design. However, do such problem-solving approaches allow sufficient space and time for understanding the complexities of cross-cultural exchange, the inherent power dynamics of which we are necessarily a part, and the sensitivities surrounding the issues at stake?

Landscape architecture is a relatively recent discipline in terms of its formal establishment. As we build and strengthen our own theoretical frameworks we look to those of other disciplines to supplement our own. That said, even more established disciplines look outside of themselves when the task at hand requires it. As landscape architects seeking more meaningful engagement with power and place, belonging and exclusion, we can look to methods used in feminist, postcolonial and queer critique. Decolonising research methodologies and critical race and whiteness studies also have useful tools. Threads common to many of these frameworks include an understanding of the politics of power, knowledge, emotion, and "reflexivity" – maintaining an awareness of ourselves on a personal and political level.

Describing how we feel and experience certain spaces, including the politics connected with these feelings and experiences, can help navigate what is often difficult terrain, without reiterating power dynamics such as whiteness and related colonial mindsets. In addition to critical race studies, alternative ways of writing about art, landscape and architecture drawing on feminist and queer phenomenologies of place offer a way in to uncovering hidden histories and disrupting our more conventional approaches to mapping and understanding place. Such strategies have been used in disciplines and contexts too numerous to mention here, but I have found Jane Rendell, Katja Grillner and Amanda Sinclair to be particularly inspiring.

Rendell coined the term "site-writing" to describe her style of reflexive writing. Site-writing deepens and extends our discussions of site specificity by incorporating the author's awareness of their own relationship to the site, the theory and ideas they are drawing on, and the place of writing itself. This complex approach combines theories of psychoanalysis with contemporary debates in art and politics, delving into the material, emotional and conceptual. It speculates on the memories, dreams and imaginings of the artist or designer, those experiencing the artwork or site, as well as the writer's own engagement with them.[5]

Grillner draws on Sara Ahmed's theorising of a queer phenomenology, Donna Harraway's situated knowledges, and other feminist architectural writings. Similar to Rendell, she explores the role of memory and everyday appropriation in place perception by using her own experience as a primary source. Grillner describes this mode of writing as performative, one that considers the role everyday appropriation and memory plays in our place perception. When we do this we are attempting to capture something of spatial perception with distraction. Therein lie important keys to understanding and knowing a particular place, the qualities or insights that are usually omitted from conventional accounts, in which the emphasis is to provide a neutral, factual, and as distanced as possible representation.[6]

Although Rendell is an art and architecture critic, there is potential to use strategies inspired by site-writing in landscape architecture, for example by supplementing case study investigations and more conventional modes of site analysis. We might term it "writing places". Similarly, used in conjunction with visual modes of representation and an awareness of the political and historical issues at hand, Grillner's approach of moving between different layers of time and lived experience offers a useful tool to landscape architects engaging with Indigenous histories.

Leadership studies academic Amanda Sinclair notes she developed a reflexive approach in her work after attending a conference themed around place with a strong guiding influence of Maori culture and knowledge in Aotearoa, New Zealand. Attendees were encouraged to think more about the impact of personal and geographic origins in their work, and how they place themselves on what they find. She suggested that any sort of work and writing is informed by a combination of internal, external, real, imagined, remembered or reconstructed places. Being more aware and explicit about this is a form of identity work that prompts important questions we don't usually ask ourselves in research, including: why am I interested in this area and how do the places I have been inform and limit what I argue for? In the context of education and research these ways of facilitating reflexive thinking about place and cultural identity, as Sinclair describes, are part of a decolonising paradigm.[7]

If we want to decolonise research, it needs to be led, designed and controlled by Indigenous communities and scholars. This control extends to the research outcomes. Academics working in this area emphasise that decolonisation is not a metaphor and as such it is different to other strategies in research, education or policy such as diversity and inclusivity.[8] Rather it refers to a specific mode of reorganising disciplinary education and practice. Views on the potential

7. Sinclair, A 2010, 'Placing Self: How Might We Place Ourselves in Leadership Studies Differently?' Leadership, vol. 6, no. 4, pp. 447-460.

8. Tuck, E, & Yang, W 2012, 'Decolonization is Not a Metaphor', Decolonization: Indigeneity, Education & Society, vol. 1, no. 1.

9. Prior, D 2007, 'Decolonising Research: a shift toward Reconciliation.' Nursing Inquiry, vol. 14, no. 2, pp. 162-168.

10. Ibid 9.

11. Smith, L 2012. Decolonizing Methodologies Research and Indigenous Peoples: 2nd ed., Zed Books, London; New York; Dunedin, N.Z.

12. Any: Architecture New York, 1996, 'Whiteness: White Forms, Forms of Whiteness,' Anyone Corporation, New York, USA, no. 16.

13. Morrison, T 1992, Playing in the Dark: Whitness and the Literary Imagination (William E. Massey Senior Lectures in the History of American Civilization), Harvard University Press, Cambridge, Mass.

for non-Indigenous involvement in decolonising research projects differ. Deborah Prior argues decolonisation is 'a collective process' that requires the engagement of both coloniser and colonised, the dominant and the marginalised.[9] Decolonising research methodologies involve the personal and the political, such as the 'critical reflexive turn' and 'shifting the agenda' within disciplines.[10] If there is to be non-Indigenous involvement in decolonising research however, agreed protocols of positionality - reflexively locating oneself in relation to the research and its outcomes - are crucial.[11] A critical understanding of Western frameworks, canons and traditions go hand in hand with individual reflexivity, based on the understanding that power operates through the production of knowledge and through individuals.

The interdisciplinary field of critical race and whiteness studies offers useful frameworks for maintaining an understanding of our own racialised positioning. This field of academic research proliferated in the United States in the 1990s in response to what was seen as a lack of substantial social change following the civil rights movement of the 1960s, although it has origins that can be traced to 1890s, par ticularly in the work and writings of W.E.B Du Bois. While it is more prevalent in the United States where it began, critical race and whiteness studies spread to Canada and across the globe to places such as Australia, predominantly through the work of Indigenous theorists and others working in Indigenous research and studies. Academics drawing on these frameworks understand whiteness to be a particular power structure operating as the accumulation of specific forms of cultural and social capital that are relevant to a particular context. Whiteness theory has been mapped on to architecture by the progressive and independent architecture magazine 'Any', not too dissimilar to Kerb, albeit with an architecture focus. 'Any' devoted an entire issue to whiteness and architecture in the 1990s.[12] Architect Mabel Wilson was one contributor who has written subsequently on the topic of race and architecture drawing on Toni Morrison's seminal text on whiteness and the literary imagination Playing in the Dark. [13]

Learning and applying tools of reflexivity is not a quick process. Realising one's own insertion into various structures of power is an ongoing commitment requiring patience, openness and the courage to make mistakes. Engaging meaningfully with the tangle of Indigenous and colonial histories involves examining our own place within the places we come to design. As landscape architects do we need to rethink our current problem-solving approach to site-specificity and inclusivity to do so?

FROM THE GROUND UP: ON REUNITING COMMUNITIES AND LANDSCAPES IN THE US-MEXICO BORDER REGION

Gabriel Díaz Montemayor

Figure 01. The proposed City of Green Creeks project. Map credit: Gabriel Díaz Montemayor and Francisco Lara Valencia)

The United States – Mexico border region is one of the most highly contested landscapes in the world today, and this is a condition that has only been exacerbated by the recent change in US federal administration. The United States - Mexico relationship is now going through one of the lows, or busts, in a seemingly perpetually multi-faceted cycle.

This is a region broadly defined by the political boundaries of its border states, in Mexico they are: Baja California, Sonora, Chihuahua, Coahuila, Nuevo León, and Tamaulipas. In the United States they are: California, Arizona, New Mexico and Texas. All of these American states are former Mexican and previously Spanish colonial territories and are still clearly visible, revealing the footprint of the pre-1848 border between the United States (US) and Mexico. This is clearly illustrated by US Census mapping of the percentage of population per county with Mexican origin ethnicity.[1]

In contrast with the current national discourse, where US federal authorities criticise Mexican policy and the Mexican government responds in its defence, local communities along the border, particularly those right on the border, face a very different daily reality. These communities experience an everyday existence of intense and fruitful economic, social and ecological cooperation between families and communities existing on both sides of the border. These are communities that benefit directly from economic success at a continental scale and on the threatened North American Free Trade Agreement (NAFTA). These communities share a stake in environmental issues which include water and air pollution, and also the qualities of riparian corridors, lush deserts, or migratory flyways for birds.

Set against a political struggle between federations, states, local communities and governments, the impassiveness of the grand landscapes of semi-arid and arid North America await a revival as a catalyst for bringing people back together. These grand landscapes are ones which have forged specific cultural

1. The Economist 2014, 'Old Mexico Lives On', viewed 14 May 2018, https://www.economist.com/news/united-states/21595434-old-mexico-lives

2. Gable, E 2010, 75 Years on, Effort to Create U.S.-Mexico Park Hampered by Security Concerns, The New York Times, viewed 10 August, 2017, https://archive.nytimes.com/www.nytimes.com/gwire/2010/06/24/24greenwire-75-years-on-effort-to-create-us-mexico-park-ha-13949.

3. Office of the Press Secretary 2010, Joint Statement from President Barack Obama and President Felipe Calderón, viewed 14 May 2018, https://obamawhitehouse.archives.gov/the-press-office/joint-statement-president-barack-obama-and-president-felipe-calder-n

identities in the region, shaping societies which have become accustomed to dealing with water scarcity and spatial isolation in stark contrast to the main centers of political and economic power. They are a frontier. The people of this border region, in their efforts to move towards a better understanding of their shared common ground, continue to struggle to counter-balance larger, more visible divisive conversations. That said, the initiatives embraced by the region's institutions, local governments and universities may have the ability to demonstrate the resilience that characterises the region.

Currently, at the larger scale of binational ecological planning, and hiding in plain sight, is the example of the binational cluster of natural parks known as the Big Bend. This area consists of the Big Bend National Park and the Big Bend Ranch State Park on the American side of the border. On the Mexican side, adjacent to these, are the Maderas del Carmen natural protected area, the flora and fauna protection area of Ocampo, and the Canon de Santa Elena National Park. These vast natural parks and protected areas offer direct precedent to binational agreements between the two countries. In 1944 then US President Franklin Roosevelt expressed to his Mexican counterpart, President Miguel Avila Camacho: 'I do not believe that this undertaking in the Big Bend [establishment of Big Bend National Park] will be complete until the entire park area in this region on both sides of the Rio Grande forms one great international park.' [2]

In 2010 presidents Barack Obama of the US and Felipe Calderón from Mexico agreed[3] on the establishment of a national area of binational interest - known as Big Bend/Rio Bravo - an achievement that underscored the need to protect the fragile desert ecosystem of this region and to preserve its unique biological diversity. The project was also viewed as a national security solution, as restricting development in the natural area was proposed to result in the mitigation of binational security concerns.

The small communities found within these natural parks rely on farming, ranching, and ecological tourism. Border security infrastructures between these parks is minimal to non-existent. In Big Bend's Boquillas port of entry, for example, there is no bridge over the river but a boat and a waiting burro (donkey) to take environmentally conscious tourists to nearby Boquillas del Carmen in Mexico, a gateway town to the Maderas del Carmen protected area. There is no border infrastructure whatsoever on the Mexican side, there is also no border wall in this stretch of the Rio Grande River in Texas.

The example of this vast natural area of binational interest demonstrates the ability of the peoples of both countries to agree and come together when it comes to their shared natural wealth. There are other latent opportunities on this vector, probably the most obvious is the Lower Rio Grande Valley stretch of the river and border found at the intersection of south Texas and the Mexican state of Tamaulipas.

On the American side exists a series of fragmented natural protected areas that comprise the Lower Rio Grande Valley National Wildlife Refuge. This stretch of the river intersects a north-south continental corridor employed by numerous migratory bird species. It is one of the best bird watching areas in the United States as birds congregate, feed and rest here on their way to the south to spend winters, and on their return to the north to spend the summers. Unfortunately, on the Mexican side there is no protected area reciprocity, with most of the riparian corridor being used for agriculture, ranching, and human settlements. Mexico could in this case actually pay for the environmental recovery of the border through the creation and management of strategically located natural protected areas and investments in urban green infrastructure networks. This has already been explored by the state government of Tamaulipas, Mexico, via commissioned urban planning and design studies[4] that leverage a forthcoming intensive exploitation of shale oil and gas resources (something that has already happened in Texas). In these, the future boom in economic development is embraced as an opportunity for environmental impact mitigation and the creation of natural protected areas on the Mexican side, operating in tandem with the American side.

A similar opportunity exists to the west, on the land border between the towns of Nogales, Sonora, and Nogales, Arizona. Also known as *Ambos Nogales*, Spanish for 'both Nogaleses'.

The river at this point flows north and the Mexican Nogales drains storm water and sewage of 250,000 people to the San Cruz River in Arizona via the Nogales creek. The Mexican Nogales pays its northern neighbours for sanitation treatment of this volume. Downtown Ambos Nogales sits at the low point of the intersection between the international border and the drainage path. Floods in the binational, but divided, downtown are a common historical occurrence. A flood that occurred in 2008 is a good example of the schism between local and federal authorities, or between national governments and local communities. During a storm, the underground and channelised Nogales creek suddenly burst in downtown Mexican Nogales from water pressure created by debris accumulated within it, aggravated by a barrier built in the channel to keep illegal migrants and merchandise from entering the United States. The local Ambos Nogales governments were unaware of the underground fence built by the US Federal Government but had to work together with them in dealing with substantial flood damage in the main commercial area of the region.

In 2010, the local municipal planning institute of Nogales, Sonora, with the support of the 'Border 2012' program of the binational Border Environment Cooperation Commission (BECC), decided to address the study of sustainable flood mitigation measures with the objective of producing high quality public space in the low-income peripheries of Nogales. This effort attempted to leverage the ongoing EPA funded construction of retention dams in the upper section of the watershed on the Mexican side and was designed to mitigate runoff volumes downstream.

The resulting project[5] proposed a public space system paired with green

4. Shearer, A, Almy, D, & Diaz Montemayor, G 2016, Integral Cities for the Tamaulipas Border Region. Report and design studio produced by the Center of Sustainable Development and the School of Architecture at The University of Texas at Austin for the State Government of Tamaulipas.

5. Lara Valencia, F, Díaz Montemayor, G 2010, City of Green Creeks: Sustainable Flood Management Alternatives for Nogales, Sonora, Arizona State University with the support of the Border 2012 Program of the Border Environment Cooperation Commission and the Municipal Planning and Research Institute of Nogales, Sonora.

Figure 02. Imagining an urban border region storm water inlet. Photomontage credit: Gabriel Díaz Montemayor

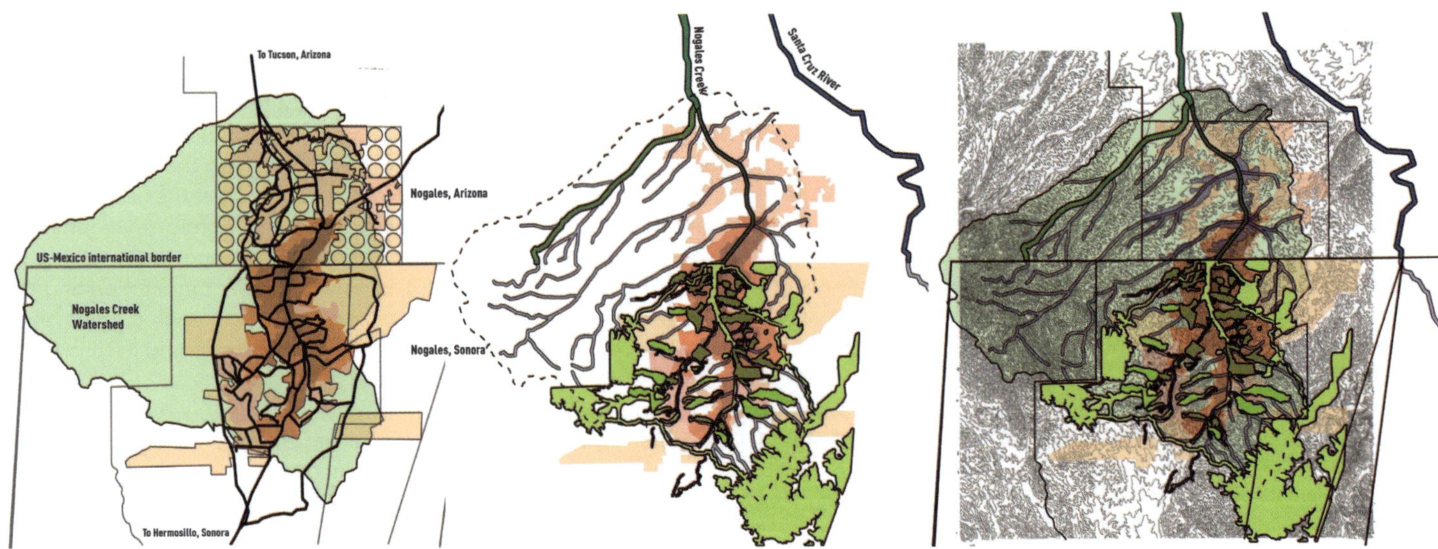

Urban structure of Ambos Nogales 2010

Green Creeks proposed Network and reshaped urban structure

Green Creeks proposed network and topographic condition

infrastructure measures. Parks aligned to creeks and drainage-ways. The proposal established a green infrastructure system distributing centrifugally from the centerline of Nogales creek towards the higher ground of the basin. It includes adaptations on the American funded water management infrastructures to reshape these as attractive public spaces in areas of high need.

Binational natural protected areas, ecologically oriented (green) infrastructure networks and the public spaces of various scales existing within all these examples exhibit a series of nested scales pertaining to different levels of governance and political responsibility. From local municipal retrofitted streets and basin-based flood management, to large scale protection of fragile ecosystems, the peoples and landscapes of the US and Mexico have a repertoire at hand to make use of and promote and if necessary recover once the current bust in the binational relationship dissipates. Unfortunately, these initiatives lie buried under a growing pile of news directed toward larger national identities and global audiences who live far away from binational rivers and the Sonoran and the Chihuahuan deserts bisected by the US Mexico border.

The projects briefly described in this essay are partnerships between American border region universities and Mexican local municipal and city governments, funded by various binational and state agencies. This mode of operation, in its specific context, tasked itself to contribute to the remediation of a vital binational relationship by serving the public good found in the environmentally and culturally rich society of the US-Mexico border region, demonstrating it is one, not two.

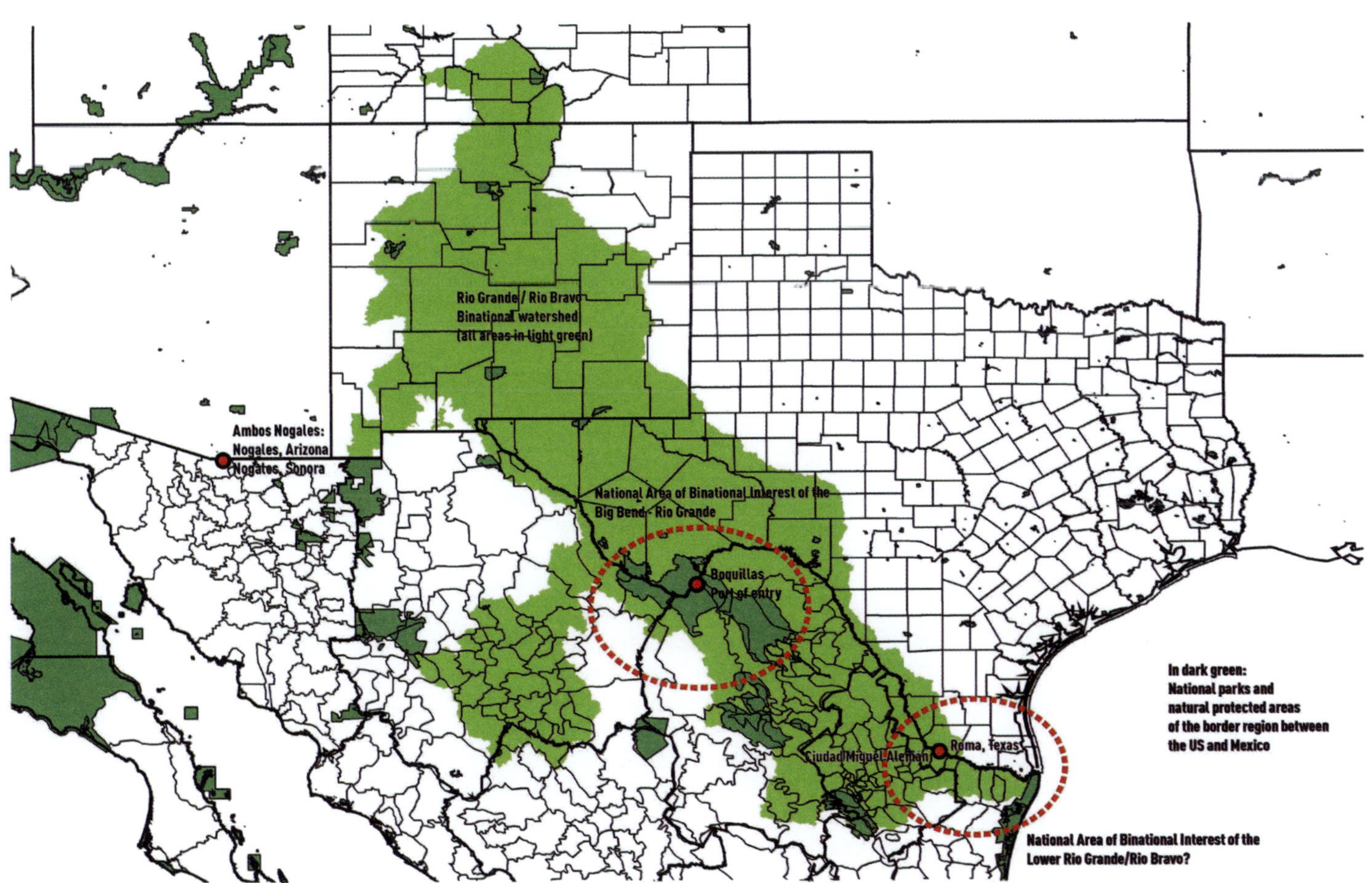

Figure 03. The border region, the binational watershed of the Rio Grande/Rio Bravo, natural parks and protected areas, existing and proposed natural areas of binational interest. Map credit: Gabriel Díaz Montemayor with information from USGS and INEGI

RE-LOCATING POSTON: DISPOSSESSION IN THE AMERICAN SOUTH-WEST

Melissa Green and Estello Raganit

Landscape is a repository of memory, both individual and collective. It is a site of and for identity ... But since memory is indelible, the struggles to preserve the landscape that represents it are intense, for while memory may be indelible people are not, and whole traditions, whole ways of knowing and being in the world can fade with the generations.

Don Mitchell,
New Axioms for Reading the Landscape:
Paying Attention to Political Economy and Social Justice.

PROLOGUE

Landscapes of war are marked by the tactical manipulation of ground conditions, including the construction of military infrastructure, and the lacerations, destructive formations and chemical traces left behind on the earth's surface. This article complicates the narrative of the landscape of war in Poston, Arizona by bringing to the fore notions of social and national identity, redefined through new boundaries and implicated in plights of power. The Poston War Relocation Center in southwest Arizona, constructed in 1942 during World War II as an internment camp for Japanese Americans, was strategically sited on the Colorado River Indian Reservation, a unilateral decision made by the United States Bureau of Indian Affairs. This siting becomes an important point of departure in studying Poston as a contested homeland of dis- or re-placement and habitation between Japanese Americans, the Colorado River Indian tribes, and national governing bodies. This investigation traces how analogous records of forced migration to the California-Arizona border serve as a vector for monumentalising site as a counter narrative of trauma for the Colorado River Indian peoples and placemaking as a form of resistance for the internment of Japanese citizens.

ACT 01

In 1865 the Chemehuevi and Mohave peoples were forced into the 432 square-mile Colorado River Indian Reservation in western Arizona following a brief series of battles in the late 1850s. Prior to this the Colorado River Indian Tribes selectively occupied a territory of roughly 200,000 square miles across the American Southwest. This forced migration transformed both the geographic and socio-cultural associations of place as well as traditional farming practices within the arid Arizona landscape.

As a result of American expansionist narratives in the nineteenth century, hundreds of thousands of Native Americans were forced into bound reserve lands, an act of ethnic cleansing. At the helm of this romanticised conquest was US President Andrew Jackson who, in his address to Congress, proclaimed 'It gives me great pleasure to announce to Congress that the benevolent policy of the Government, steadily pursued for nearly thirty years, in relation to the removal of the Indians beyond the white settlements is approaching a happy consummation'.[1] Jackson ends the address with a declaration that it is by the good graces of the US Government that land would be apportioned to the Native American peoples, framing the formation of the Colorado River Indian Reservation.

Ireteba, a Mohave Sub-chief, and Charles Poston, Arizona's Superintendent of Indian Affairs, travelled along the Colorado River to determine the site of the Colorado River Indian Reservation in the upper Colorado Valley. Contrary to Chief Ireteba's original recommendations, the reservation was located on unwanted territory where

1. Jackson, A. 1830, On Indian Removal, 2nd Session to 21st Congress, Washington, D.C., 1830.

2. Caylor, A 2000, 'A Promise Long Deferred: Federal Reclamation on the Colorado River Indian Reservation', Pacific Historical Review, vol. 69, no. 2, pp. 193–215.

3. Okimoto, R Y 2001, Sharing a Desert Home: Life on Colorado River Indian Reservation, Poston, Arizona, 1942-1945. Heyday Books, Berkeley, CA.

4. Exec. Order. No. 9066, 7 Fed. Reg. 1407, 25 February, 1942, viewed November 2018, https://www.archives.gov/federal-register/executive-orders/1942.html

5. Eaton, A H 1952, Beauty Behind Barbed Wire, Harper , New York.

6. Bailey, P 1971, City in the Sun, Westernlore Press , Los Angeles.

7. Ibid. 6.

river flow patterns were more erratic and soils less fertile.[2] Historically, seasonal flooding patterns decided the river banks that Chemehuevi and Mohave peoples inhabited; they subsisted via mosaic farmlands along the broad, alluvial bottomlands of the Colorado River. Water availability and unfavorable soil conditions became the source of contestation. To avoid offering annuities to the native peoples, the US Government promised to establish a robust irrigation system on newly sited reserve lands, ensuring annual crop yields. This action forced a permanent type of settlement and replaced the Colorado River tribes' traditional semi-nomadic lifestyle with Eurocentric ideas of stasis.

The reservation imposed a new, bound conception of space. Previously the Mohave and Chemehuevi people actively referenced geographic features – including landmarks such as Black Canyon and Avi kwame (Spirit Mountain) – as a means of identifying fertile areas and ancestral lands.[3] Their temporal occupation along the Colorado River, informed by traditional ecological knowledge of regular seasonal flooding, was replaced with the challenges of an imposed infrastructural system. A series of canals, dams, and levees were constructed, channelising the river and drastically altering the Native Americans' agricultural relationship with it.

The new geographic boundaries of reserve lands were emblematic of a lost subsistence practice, a fleeting cultural memory. These physical constraints demanded a spatial perspective that challenged the Colorado River Indians' understanding of land, home, and self-identity. The confines of the reservation lands became a traumatic reminder of cultural erasure. Once a space of mobility, home became fixed, a site of oppression.

ACT 02

On 19 February 1942, President Franklin Delano Roosevelt directed the Secretary of War to establish a series of military zones to confine all Japanese Americans. This action, following Japan's attack on Pearl Harbor, was intended to implement 'every possible protection against espionage and against sabotage to nation-defense material'.[4] The attack on Pearl Harbor ushered in a wave of fear and discrimination in the US against people of Japanese ancestry. Within a week of the call for the immediate evacuation of 'all persons of Japanese lineage', the United States Western Defense Command established the War Relocation Authority (WRA).[5] Japanese Americans were forced out of their homes and sent to camps, constructed on remote desert landscapes, where they were met with barracks lined with barbed wire fences, sentry towers, and soldiers outfitted with machine guns.[6]

As a result of this legislation over 17,000 Japanese Americans from southern California were interned at the Poston Relocation Center in Poston, Arizona, one of the largest Japanese internment camps in the US. The WRA initially hesitated with establishing the site because of its location within the Colorado River Indian Reservation – the local Colorado River tribal councils refused to accept the project as it was too familiar to their own experiences of forced migration.[7] Nevertheless, the Bureau of Indian Affairs argued that the labour by the Japanese Americans would assist in expanding the degrading irrigation and agricultural infrastructure that had plagued the Colorado River Indians since the reservation's initial siting. The Bureau of Indian Affairs overruled the tribal council's appeals.[8]

The wild desert landscape of Poston, Arizona sits on a flat basin east of the Colorado River in one of the hottest and driest areas in the country. Nevertheless, Japanese traditions and culture bloomed. The internees manipulated their new environment, subverting their captivity through the preservation of tradition and making a home where it did not exist. Months after arrival, the relocation camp, which mirrored master plans of military bases, prisons, and farmhouses, saw punctuations of social landscape elements, signs of both resilience and resistance.

Between the barracks and at major entrances appeared gardens equipped with bridges and water features that were sown with seeds carried in the pockets of internees.[9] The garden spaces, inspired by traditional Japanese landscape techniques and adjusted to the desert climate, represented the prisoners' desires to connect to their new environments and foster a sense of community. The gardens also allowed for social spaces to emerge amid the suffocating barrack conditions. The Issei (first-generation Japanese immigrants) constructed a temple, a fragile and brightly-colored structure radiating in contrast to the homogenous desert landscape. The temple encouraged community gathering and created an accessible space to practice spirituality and share religious and cultural traditions. Though the desert conditions eliminated any possibility for the use of colourful flowers in traditional ceremonies, hand-crafted flowers emerged, fabricated using origami on brightly-coloured papers. This action illustrates the prisoner's eagerness to break up the monotony of the desert and recreate a semblance of their Californian homes. Shinto and tea societies were also established, and an old-world bathhouse materialised in defiance against the humiliating public showers and multiple holed latrines.[10]

These landscape insertions illuminate the internees' desire to not only persist in the harsh desert environment but also resist the imposing, imprisoning state apparatus. The vernacular interventions functioned as significant cultural and social markers during these warring times, to affect spaces of community and analogs of home.

ACT 03

Following the three and a half years of Japanese internment, the Poston landscape - a site already embedded with tension following the displacement of the Colorado River Indian Tribes - had become a cumulative palimpsest of trauma, memory, and identity. Poston had become the unwanted home of two cultures dispossessed. Presently, the landscape at Poston reveals just as much as it conceals. The landscape ruins (the abandoned internment camp barracks and the irrigation systems) mask the collective memory of this counter narrative, separated in time, but tied together in space.

Currently a monument stands among the ruins of the abandoned camp, commemorating the 'men, women, and children who suffered countless hardships and indignities at the hands of a nation misguided by wartime hysteria, racial prejudice, and fear'.[11] The thirty-foot concrete obelisk, which emerges from a Japanese stone lantern, is encircled by palm trees. Though the memorial attempts to re-locate and commemorate the Japanese experience, it neglects the equally persistent trauma of the Colorado River Indian tribes before it. Thus, the War Relocation Center at Poston, Arizona is a site of layered tragedies. The town stands as a result of two analogous accounts of cultural marginalisation - one under the guise of national conquest, the other, national security. Analysis of the town's past critiques notions of home as they relate to the cultural memory of these two shared geographic histories of dispossession.

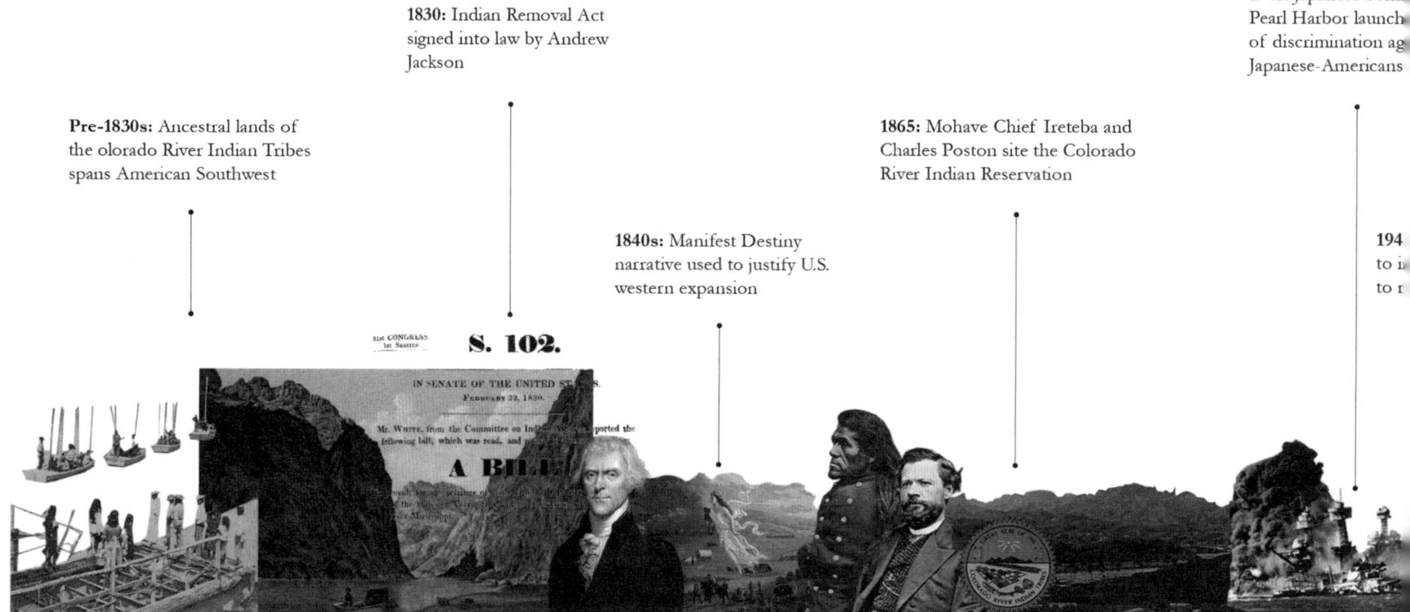

Act 01, *A Happy Consummation*

8. Fujita-Rony, T 2015, Poston (Colorado River), Densho Encyclopedia, viewed 11 May 2018, https://encyclopedia.densho.org/Poston%20(Colorado%20River)/.

9. Matsuoka, J 1974, Camp 11, Block 211, Daily Life in an Internment Camp, Japan Publications, Inc. San Francisco.

10. Bailey, P 1971, City in the Sun, Westernlore Press, Los Angeles.

11. 'Poston Memorial Monument' 1992, Monument inscription, Poston, Arizona, USA.

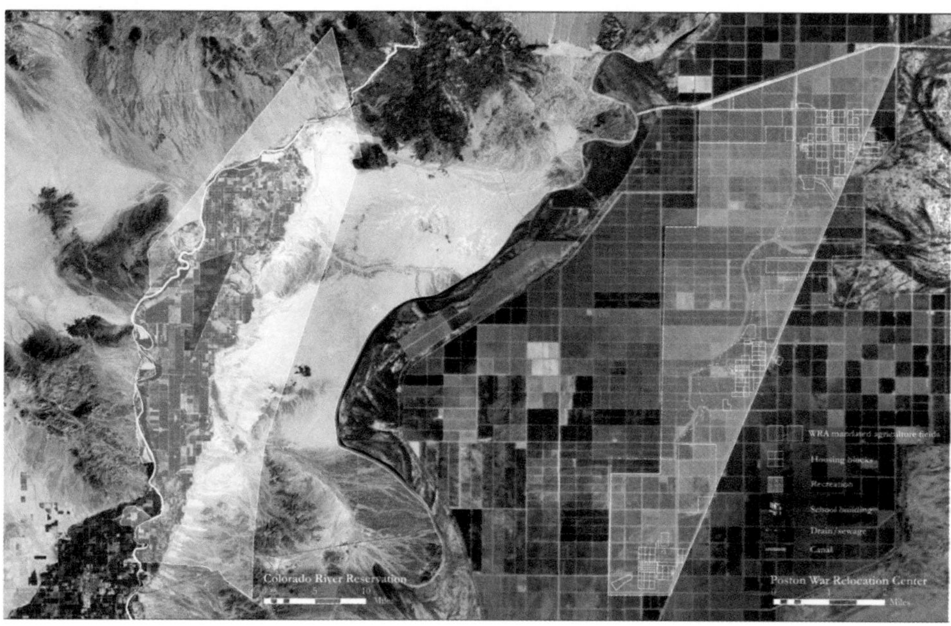

1945: Relocation camp at Poston closes following the end of World War II

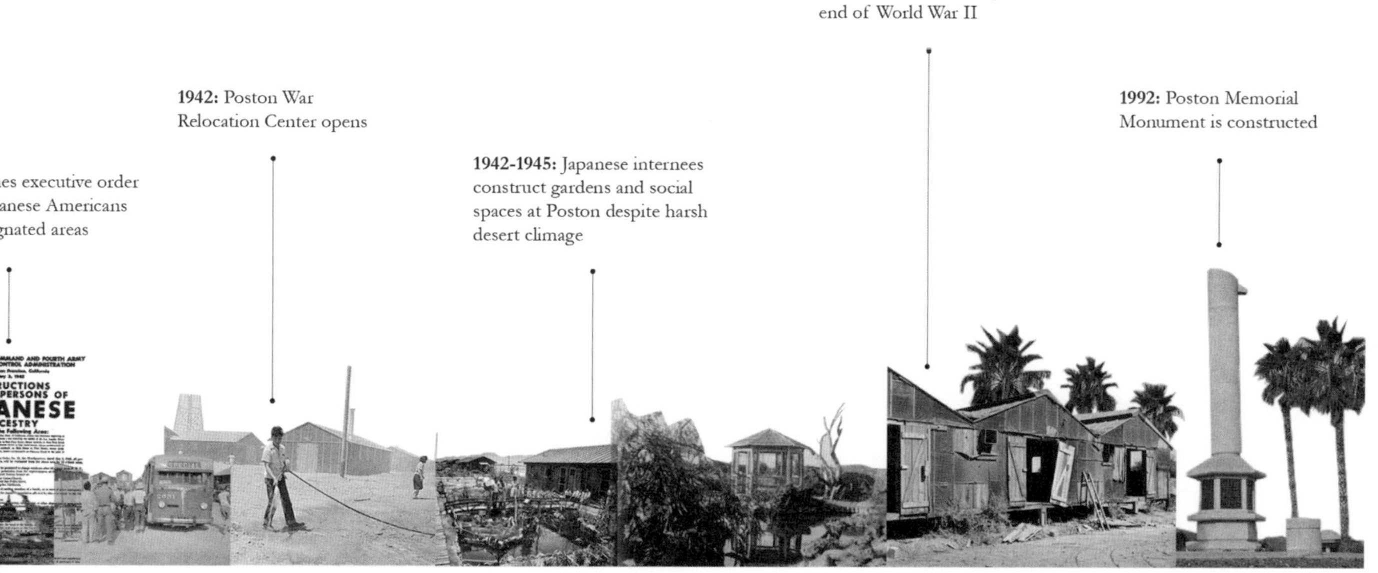

Act 01, *Enforced Compliance*

Act 03, *The Remnants*

MAPPING THE MASSACRES OF AUSTRALIA'S COLONIAL FRONTIER

Frontier Massacre Research Team

The use of online mapping tools to construct historical narratives from sources, usually hidden in dusty archives, is an important innovation for academic historians. In the past, incidents of frontier massacre were often denied, leaving the general public confused about the reliability of sources. The digital mapping tool developed by Professor Lyndall Ryan and her research team at the University of Newcastle, for Stage 1 of their project titled: Colonial Frontier Massacres in Australia, 1788 to 1960 is one of the first to make these sources available to the general public. Stage 1, known as Colonial Frontier Massacres in Eastern Australia 1788 to 1872, was launched in July 2017.

For Stage 1, the project team developed a process that allowed them to use the online map as a narrative. This process enables map users to query the sources and analyse the data for dispersion of the frontier massacre sites, and how, when and why they occurred. What distinguishes this online map from others currently available is the development of a coherent methodology and criteria that can be used to determine what constitutes a frontier massacre. The online map developed by Culture Victoria for example, identifies a number of frontier massacre sites in Victoria but provides no definition of a frontier massacre.[1] The website, Australians Together, mentions frontier massacres in general as part of colonisation and dispossession but lacks details of individual incidents.[2] Others show a static map of incidents with lists of links to newspaper articles,[3] while some detailed frontier massacre websites are now broken links.

The first step in the process of collecting the narratives of frontier massacres and transforming them into data for upload to the map involved converting records from conventional text-based storage systems into a formal structured database using Excel and Google Sheets systems. Content was grouped into thirty-five common fields of information that retained the narrative detail yet isolated key elements of each massacre including language group of the victims and number killed. Also included were the perpetrator names, their motive, time of day of the attack and the weapons they used. The massacre site stories were then reformatted into a Geographic Information System (GIS) layer that became the core of the online map. The map, created by Bill Pascoe using the ArcGIS JavaScript API, was embedded as one page of the website and the associated site records were stored in a database.

1. Massacre Map 2016, Culture Victoria, viewed 26 May 2018, <https://cv.vic.gov.au/stories/aboriginal-culture/indigenous-stories-about-war-and-invasion/massacre-map/ > .

2. What About History? n.d., Australians Together, viewed 26 May 2018, <https://www.australianstogether.org.au/discover/australian-history/get-over-it/>.

3. Geogatos, G 2013, 'The killing times', The Stringer Independent News, viewed 26 May 2018, <http://thestringer.com.au/the-killing-times-2214#.WKrXeW996UI>.

4. Mann, B 2013, 'Fractal massacres in the old Northwest: the example of the Miamis', Journal of Genocide Research, vol. 15, no. 2, pp. 172.

5. Semelin, J 2001, 'In consideration of massacre', Journal of Genocide Research, vol. 3 no. 3, pp. 377-389.

6. Ryan, L 2010, 'Settler massacres on the Port Phillip Frontier 1836–1851', Journal of Australian Studies, vol. 34, no. 3, pp. 257-273.

7. Ryan, L 2018, Colonial Frontier Massacres in Central and Eastern Australia 1788-1930, viewed 30 July 2018, https://c21ch.newcastle.edu.au/colonialmassacres/ .

The website shows a fully navigable national map of frontier massacres. Clicking on an individual site shows summary details including a narrative description, which is often a personal account. Full details, including a three dimensional scene of the landscape, are available. The progression of the massacres over time is shown via an adjustable timeline widget.

Early website metrics indicate that the site is of great interest to Australians, has a global reach, and demonstrate that historical material is no longer confined to a niche group of academic historians or particular interest groups. The advantage of an online mapping tool is that it can be updated at regular intervals, allowing the inclusion of new material and corrections.

The primary goal of the project is to identify and locate frontier massacres using strict criteria to define massacre and its manifestations. Inclusion of reliable sources and numbers killed is based on conservative estimates. The project team has drawn on Ryan's previous work and international scholars of massacre, such as Jacques Semelin and Barbara Alice Mann, to define a frontier massacre in Australia as the killing of six or more undefended people in one operation.[4,5] Given that most Aboriginal mobs consist of twenty to thirty people, a thirty per cent loss 'leads to the whole community collapsing'.[6]

Each massacre site was graded according to the reliability and robustness of the evidence. Once selected the next task was to locate the site on the ground based on landmarks and directions from available sources. The team made extensive use of old maps such as Land Map and Land Grant maps. For example, 'the spot where the skirmish took place, in the rear of Mr David Murray's farm, at the Elizabeth River' ... 'Having seen their fires in a gully near the river'.[7] A mix of new features within GIS aided the task. This process meant that the coordinates were collated from a variety of map sources with their associated variety of data and projections.

Other problems with correctly locating sites included the reality that water courses move over time, so a spatially accurate location may position the site outside the original context. For example, a frontier massacre that occurred at the east side of the river may now be on the west side of the river because of changes wrought by floods over a century or more. For this reason, the historical narratives do not always align with present day descriptions of the location. There is a tension between describing the location in its historical context, on the west side of the river, or as it is now on the east side. However, this problem was minimised by the fact the geographic points have been made purposefully imprecise to around 250 metres, in order to protect the sites from desecration. Frontier massacre sites are shown in an indicative location deliberately blurred to make it difficult to find the exact site. The inherent map error in the collection process is negligible as massacres occurred over a broad area, such as a campsite or sometimes pursuits. The area over which massacres occurred is generally larger than any margin of error allowed for in the precision of points and areas marked on the map.

The current research team consists of two historians, a digital humanities expert and a digital cartographer.[i] The need for specialist input required coordination and planning. In hindsight if we were to start the project again we would engage the cartographer and the IT personnel at an earlier stage in the project. The cartographer would review the data collation process while the historians would learn the technical process. Each of us now has a better understanding of the requirements of digital cartography and web maps, and we are better prepared for Stage 2 and 3 of the project. The technical members have a better understanding of the historical evaluation process and the vagaries of historical information, and the historians have a better understanding of the advanced features of Excel, Google Sheets and data management. The experience of working in a multidisciplinary team has given each of us new insights into research methods and practices in a digital world.

As a historian, the visual animation provided by the timeline ruler conveyed to Jennifer Debenham the rapid pastoral expansion from Tasmania to Victoria, and through western New South Wales to the -west regions of Queensland. This process helped Jennifer to better understand the economic drivers of colonial expansion. As a cartographer, Mark Brown developed a greater understanding of the complexity of colonial dispossession.

From our experience working on this project it is clear that digital mapping is a powerful tool and will play a key role in the next step of research and teaching Australian history. Digital mapping GIS analysis provides a quick method to test and evaluate interpretive theories of history, richly adding to the historical narrative.

The visual capacity of the mapping tool provides a physical dimension to the historical narrative of Australia's colonial past. The site for Stage 1 provides a platform that has the potential to create dialogue around space and identity. The ability to visually locate sites of frontier massacre of Aboriginal people, by the invading pastoralists and other colonists, leaves the visitor to the map in no doubt that the process of Aboriginal dispossession was violent and lethal. That colonists found it necessary to resort to this kind of extreme violence to take the land demonstrates that Aboriginal people did not willingly leave or cooperate, but strongly resisted the invasion. Stage 2 and 3 of the map will show the pattern of violence spread out from eastern Australia across the whole of Australia well into the 20th century.

Overall the response to the map is very positive. In particular many Aboriginal people and communities have welcomed the site because of the way it demonstrates violence of the colonial frontier in Australia. The site not only overturns the long-held view that Australia was settled peacefully by British colonists and that Aboriginal people simply "faded away" over time, it also shows how frontier massacres were a critical component in the British conquest of Australia.

••

i. A project of this magnitude, time length and originality will always undergo changes in research personnel and shifts in focus in methodology, data collection and presentation. The ARC funded the project because it sought to represent the past in ways that had never been done before. So, it's not surprising that for every member of the research team the project has been a steep learning curve. We had never worked together before and each of had to learn new concepts. This is what makes the project so important and ground breaking. We should see ourselves as pioneers in an exciting new field rather than beating ourselves up for not knowing at the outset, exactly how to do the project.

The online map raises issues about the existing tensions between belonging and exclusion in Australia. Aboriginal people have never relinquished sovereignty of their homelands yet their ability to physically occupy traditional Country is still often denied. This has occurred through urban development and expansion, industry, agriculture and commerce, and enforcement of a foreign legal system that continues to deny their rights to occupy the land, once solely the domain of their ancestors. The story of belonging of Country, to Aboriginal people and the dispossession of it, is a vital part of the Australian story. This map helps tell that story.

Although it is becoming more accepted that many Aboriginal people were killed by the invading colonists, there is a preference to think of frontier violence as a few isolated, unfortunate and rare incidents; perhaps the sort of run-ins that are only to be expected from wild colonial boys after they've had a few (drinks), or the callous crimes of just one or two ruthless men, rather than being recurrent acts of deliberate brutal extermination. The seven known sites of frontier massacres of colonial invaders are well documented and marked with a memorial or plaque. This is rarely the case for many of the sites of frontier massacres of Aboriginal people. Indeed some of the sites are still highly contested, such as the site at Risdon Cove on the outskirts of Hobart in Tasmania. Those who deny there was a massacre at Risdon Cove question: whether it should be called a "massacre", the plausibility of evidence, the exact position of the site and the numbers actually killed.

Reprisal killings by the military and settlers for murder, by Aboriginal peoples of shepherds or stockmen, was common. In an 1826 incident on the Bridgeman Estate at Fal Brooke in the Hunter Valley, New South Wales, a party of stockkeepers and police, led by a local magistrate, murdered at least eighteen Aboriginal people in reprisal for the alleged Aboriginal killing of two shepherds.

The online map contains a comments section that encourages feedback about each of the narratives and suggestions about where and when other frontier massacres occurred. The comments assist in the team's ongoing research. The majority of comments come from people living in regional areas, indicating that frontier massacres play a greater role in local regional history narratives compared to the interests of city dwellers.

Made by whitefellas to inform whitefellas about the violence of the colonial frontier, the success of the frontier massacres' website demonstrates the effectiveness of using maps to present little known or contested historical narratives. There is something very tangible about being able to physically show where and when massacres occurred. They can not only be seen as individual incidents but also as part of a much wider campaign of extermination. The research team hope the mapping tool will generate a greater awareness and acknowledgement of the violent history of pastoral invasion across Australia and help vindicate stories about violence that Aboriginal ancestors suffered through the colonisation process.

The project to research and build this frontier massacres online map is led by historian, Professor Lyndall Ryan at the University of Newcastle in consultation with The Wollotuka Institute and AIATSIS. This site is supported by the Centre For The History Of Violence and the Centre For 21st Century Humanities. This research was funded by the Australian Government through the Australian Research Council, Project Id: DP140100399.

ENGAGING COLLABORATIVELY

IN CONVERSATION

Jefa Greenaway

KERB: As you know, the theme for our issue is HOMELANDS. We would like to know where you from are and what kind of a relationship do you have with your homeland?

Jefa Greenaway: My mob is Wailwan / Kamilaroi which is in north-western New South Wales. My father grew up on Coroona Mission which is just south of Tamworth. But I've never lived on Country so, as is frequently the case for Indigenous people or those who have Indigenous heritage, there is often a dislocation with their traditional lands.

I was born in Sydney, grew up on the Central Coast but have lived on Kulin Nation Country for the last thirty-five years. There is often a complex relationship to one's Country and the reality is that you may not be physically located on Country but you can also still maintain a connection. That can be a connection through kin, family, memory or exploration in terms of finding ways to re-establish or maintain connection. In many respects I thought to explore that through practice, research and other means; invariably it's something that can resonate particularly when I'm doing projects which have a strong Indigenous flavour or interface. I seek to try and draw on those connections as a way of going back through time and place to reference an understanding of Country.

KERB: Why did you want to become an architect? Where do your influences come from?

JG: The starting point really was a desire to artistically communicate or find a means for cultural expression. I often say that a lot of it stems from the ability to draw. But further to that there has to be a sort immediacy of mind to hand; to quickly and intuitively communicate through drawing and developing that process to distil, and then transfer an idea, whether it's through drawing, making physical models, etc.

So that's where my interest sort of stems from and also maybe from having creative people in the family. My grandfather was quite an established draftsperson. He could draw particularly well in a technical sense. My mother was trained in communication design and my sister is an artist. So it's part of our DNA.

Ngarara Place RMIT Universty. Greenaway Architects. In collaboration with Indigenous landscape designer Charles Solomon. Decal artwork by Aroha Groves.

KERB: Does being the only registered Indigenous architect in Victoria make you feel under pressure? Do you think it has an effect on your work?

JG: It's more an acute sense of responsibility. Having the privilege and the opportunity to go through the depth of study that is involved in architecture, there's a sense of need to give back, and that's in many reasons why I maintain a connection through the academy and maintain a foot in both camps. As a practitioner I've always paralleled that with having a role with the University of Melbourne. It is really about passing on knowledge, communicating and giving back to a place where I have essentially developed a lot of my thinking and skills. It is also to showcase, role model, and mentor with other practitioners and younger members of the practice, particularly students. That is in part why we set up Indigenous Architecture and Design Victoria (IADV) is a not-for-profit organisation that we (Rueben Berg and I) set up back in 2010. Our remit was to look at ways to empower and showcase (particularly Indigenous people) the value of being involved within the built environment profession; to communicate (particularly to industry) the value of incorporating Indigenous knowledge systems as part of the mix in how we think about place making; and to showcase to Indigenous communities the value of what good design thinking can offer in terms of realising their aspirations. With that in mind, what we've sought to do over the years is to engage within the public realm; facilitate lateral pathways into universities; provide opportunities for younger members; and also get to a point where ultimately we can pass the baton on to younger members coming through.

So, there's not so much a sense of a pressure per se, but more a sense of responsibility of what opportunities I've been given that enable using the skills and capacities I've developed over time, which can be used for the benefit of community when we're invited to contribute.

KERB: How do you see the architectural education and practice changing in Australia into the future?

JG: What we are starting to see now is a fundamental shift. The shift is really centered on developing methods and processes which embed Indigenous content into curricula, and this is in large part my role, currently, at the University of Melbourne. To be specific, I look at curriculum development, and Indigenising the curriculum for want of a better description. What this essentially offers is the capacity to normalise a connection with the oldest continuing culture in the world and showcase the deep knowledge of place, Country and connections. It is something that everyone has the opportunity to think about, and that Indigenous culture is something that we all share. It is a real possibility to celebrate and move beyond the deficit discourse that is often connected to this culture; to say that Indigenous culture is not static but is a lived culture and something that is constantly evolving and adapting. You don't survive on this vast continent, and its hostile environment, without the ability to adapt and change.

KERB: In a broad sense, what would you say about the gap that we see in Australia at the moment between architecture for Indigenous people and architecture by Indigenous people? Are there things in particular that need to be remedied in that area?

JG: The reality is, there is little work that occurs by Indigenous people within the built environment and that's simply a reality of the metrics.

But there is an emerging cohort that is evolving and starting to stake their claim, developing a cohesive voice, showcasing different ways of thinking and different opportunities existing.

For Aboriginal (and Torres Strait Islander) people this is another aspect that has its own challenges, particularly considerations around whether one has sufficient skills, capacities and/or resources to engage in development opportunities. It comes to, what I often call, cultural intelligence or cultural humility, where non-Indigenous practitioners who have the skill and wherewithal to navigate the complexities or sensitivities, and also understand some of the due process or protocol.

If you haven't had any exposure to Indigenous culture it's very hard for you to engage in that space because you don't necessarily have the understanding. So, naturally enough, there's a role to play for Indigenous interlocutors or facilitators to act as a conduit to enable people to navigate projects which have a strong Indigenous interface. The reality being: everyone has a potential role to play because there are far too many projects that have an Indigenous aspect for Indigenous practitioners to undertake. So, it's really about empowering others to go on a learning journey to build up their skills so they may equally contribute, but understand that in an ideal world such projects, will in time, become Indigenous led. This is very much part of the understanding of a process which ideally becomes culturally responsive. What better way than to have Indigenous people front, centre and deeply embedded as part of a project?

KERB: Quite a few people talk about how there aren't many big Indigenous Cultural Centres in Australia's major cities and how these are kept more to regional areas. Do you have any thoughts on why that is the way things are at the moment?

JG: It's a multifaceted question to think about. I think on one level a lot of it is really about generating opportunities and employment in regional centres and connecting into places where there is an intensification of an Indigenous populace. It is about drawing on the local.

Then there are also the challenges of how one represents a sort of a pan-Indigenous consideration because when we look at the Aboriginal map of Australia it's made up of over 250 discrete language groups and what it acknowledges is there's a huge diversity across the rich tapestry that is Aboriginal Australia.

So, when we start thinking about having a purpose built facility that showcases a breadth of Indigenous identity and culture, it becomes quite a challenging design proposition. Not to say that we shouldn't be going down that path exploring those possibilities, like we've seen through recent design projects, for example a contemporary gallery competition in Adelaide. These have peaked over a number of years, particularly over the last two decades, where different propositions have arisen about these as an idea. The tricky aspect here is really looking at the how and whom does one engage with. So, there are layers here that one needs to navigate and in many respects this is why it hasn't been fully embraced or realised.

In addition, there're always limitations around budgets. You need people who have a financial commitment and you need champions to push an idea and advocate for it because these things don't just happen. They can take a decade from the start of the initial conception of an idea to the realisation. So there are many aspects along the way.

KERB: In a recent article in Architecture Australia, you talked about how the relocation of the Koorie Heritage Trust to accommodate an Apple store, 'facilitates a unique opportunity for a large multinational like apple to meaningfully engage with indigenous community in the spirit of reconciliation'.

Compared to much of the social discussion around this project, you seem to have taken a very optimistic stance on this. Could you expand a little bit on how specifically you hope Apple will "engage" in the manner you suggest?'

JG: Well naturally we're talking about a global player, a massive organisation. So there is often a tendency with these big organisations to be quite homogeneous or to have a "one size fits all" approach. But I guess in terms of the relationship to Indigenous culture, particularly here, we're connected to the oldest continuing culture in the world and there's a lot of knowledge and understanding at play.

What better way to connect to the location of a major brand than to actually reference where you're locating it? So I think that this provides a unique opportunity to infuse a project with a sensibility which very much connects to place. This type of place-centred approach is something that I'm quite interested in and it's fair to say that connection to Country is the common thematic which unifies Indigenous people across this country. We also know that through corporations, colonisation and imperialism, there has been a disenfranchisement of Indigenous peoples; these propositions can in some way start to talk to that complexity and can become an exemplary model of a process which empowers everybody but uniquely centres Indigenous voices as part of a major intervention in a city like Melbourne. These ideas can potentially become a catalyst.

We understand the realities of capitalism, but when it comes to the actual design idea we see an international architectural firm undertaking work in Melbourne. But that location has real resonance because of its Indigenous relationship. Having been involved in the design of the original Koorie Heritage Trust at Federation Square in the Yarra Building, I intimately understand the importance of that place because the whole genesis of our idea and design was to reference place and connect to the Birrarung (Yarra river). Adjacent to the Koorie Heritage Trust site is the river and it resonates through time, talks to the occupation on its banks, and to an actual crossing point on the river used to connect the different Kulin nations . It is no accident that some of the significant places we know and love today were also significant places in Aboriginal history. The MCG was a corroboree ground or place that unified the Kulin nations and has always been a gathering place. There are stories to tell in understanding connection to place and this approach very much acknowledges that understanding: of how one can imbue a project with a particular sensibility which can offer uniqueness.

KERB: With the growing pressure for social/ political reform in contemporary Australia. (Uluru statement from the heart/ pressure for constitutional representation), how would you recommend architects and designers hoping to take part in this process move forward?

JG: My father spent ten years working on the '67 referendum, and these things don't happen quickly. There has to be a political will. Having also studied politics, I have a continued interest in political machinations and how politics can change things for the better. I've always advocated that in many respects architecture has a duty to become more political and use that agency to facilitate change. But I'm equally optimistic and understand that in Victoria the culture is slightly different. We are, for instance, talking about treaty. We also challenge things around how we celebrate and on what day, at the municipal council level. We have very strong Indigenous voices that are quite prepared to have a conversation and engage within the public realm.

So I don't see it as being at all daunting or problematic. I see capacities and opportunities and I think that we've yet to see the younger cohort coming through, who are quite savvy and have the ability to use some of the systems, processes and technologies to their advantage. But I think that it's an imperative for those of us who are deeply embedded in the design fraternity to advocate, agitate and seek meaningful change. We can use that voice and platform to do things in such a way that essentially will leave a legacy and improve our lot. Things are a little bit better because of our contribution and we have a role to play, and a responsibility to challenge things which may not be as we want them to be. We need to do that methodically and with intelligence. We need to use systems to our advantage to manage this change. We need to demonstrate the valuable propositions of Aboriginal people's contribution within this sector. But that said, we know that politics is a fickle beast and I think that the limitations of parliamentary terms reinforces that the cycles are quite short. So it's often a difficult proposition, but when we start to work together with a collective mindset we can start to develop strategies that become positive enablers of change.

CLIMATE CHANGE NARRATIVES IN THE NEGEV DESERT

Melanie Li

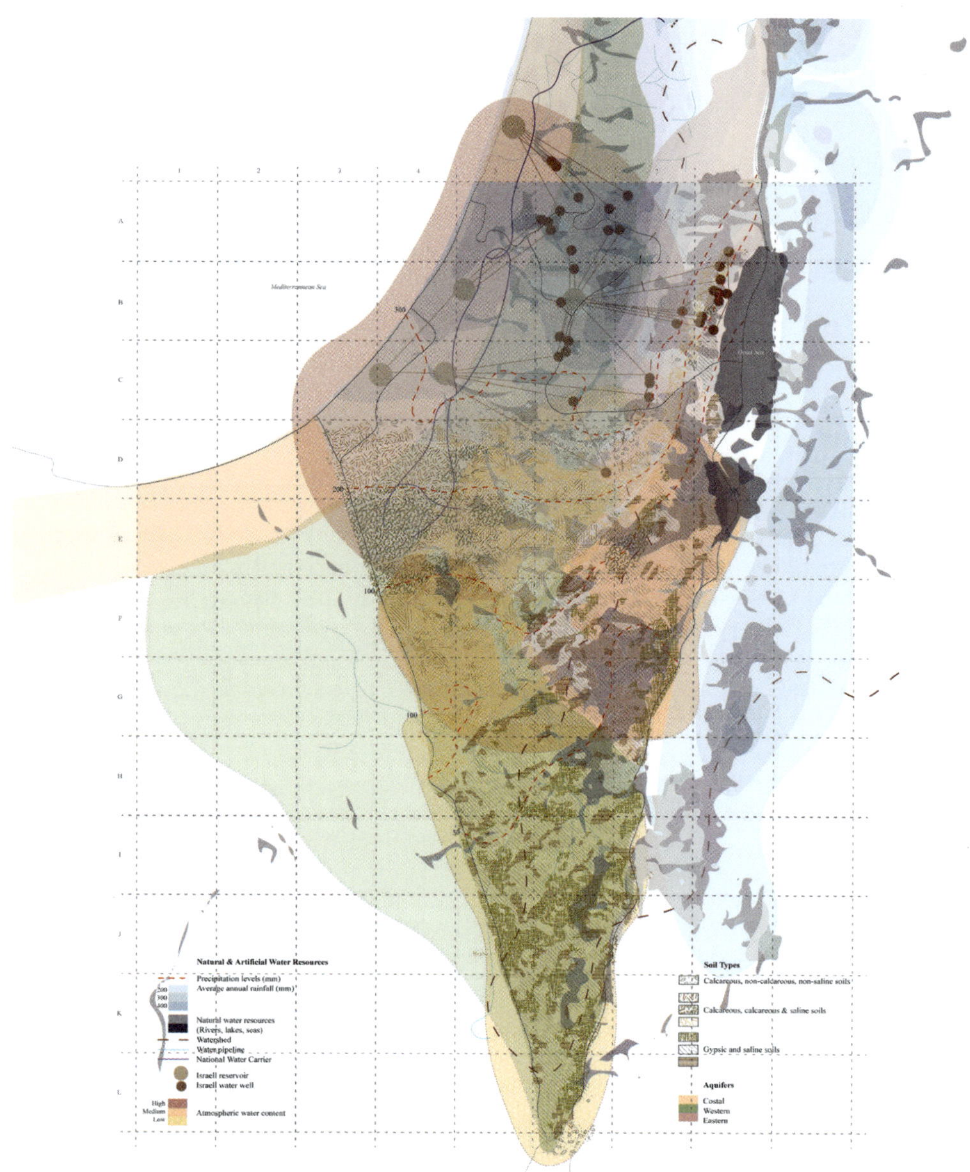

This project deals with the desert of the Negev/Naqab by exploring its landscape through the experiential and programmatic opposites of sand and water. The current landscape, known to be inhabited by Bedouin settlements, is otherwise recognised as fragmented by the socio-political implications brought upon by continuous colonial contestation. Likewise, the varying climate conditions evident in the northern and southern regions of the land, along with the gradual increase in global temperatures, bring forth questions regarding the future state of this desert landscape.

The intervention therefore questions established assumptions and images of the desert, including the fraught but essential nature of dialogue, exchange and understanding. The landscape was first interpreted through a series of critical mappings, formulated in order to curiously understand its crux. Moreover, the issue of "water" was treated as the lens through which the desert was mapped, to further grasp any social, economic, or political undertones implicit in the way the Negev is perceived. As a critique to the implications of colonialism brought upon the land and the people, an apocalyptic narrative was imagined; a landscape exhausted by depleted aquifers and extreme heat.

Waterskin Base 008 is one of multiple water bases offered within the proposed dystopian future. This water intervention acts as a first initiative for underground inhabitation, as the surface landscape increasingly deteriorates. A series of solar stills fill natural ground holes formed from the cracking land, providing water to the people of Negev, utilising the heat to supplement natural evaporation and condensation processes. Connected to each solar still is a system of pipes that routes the water to an artificial aquifer beneath the surface. Citizen scientists and underground workers monitor the aquifer and manage water production levels, in an effort to strengthen the community through a collective program. Above, nomadic groups and communities travel from base to base, amassing the resources necessary for their survival in an unmerciful landscape.

Solar stills cover ground holes, create water to supply aquifer, and filter light into underground caves
Entrance
Pressure pump helps route water from aquifer to wells
Well 01
Durable plastic flap covers well opening
Solar panels power pressure pump

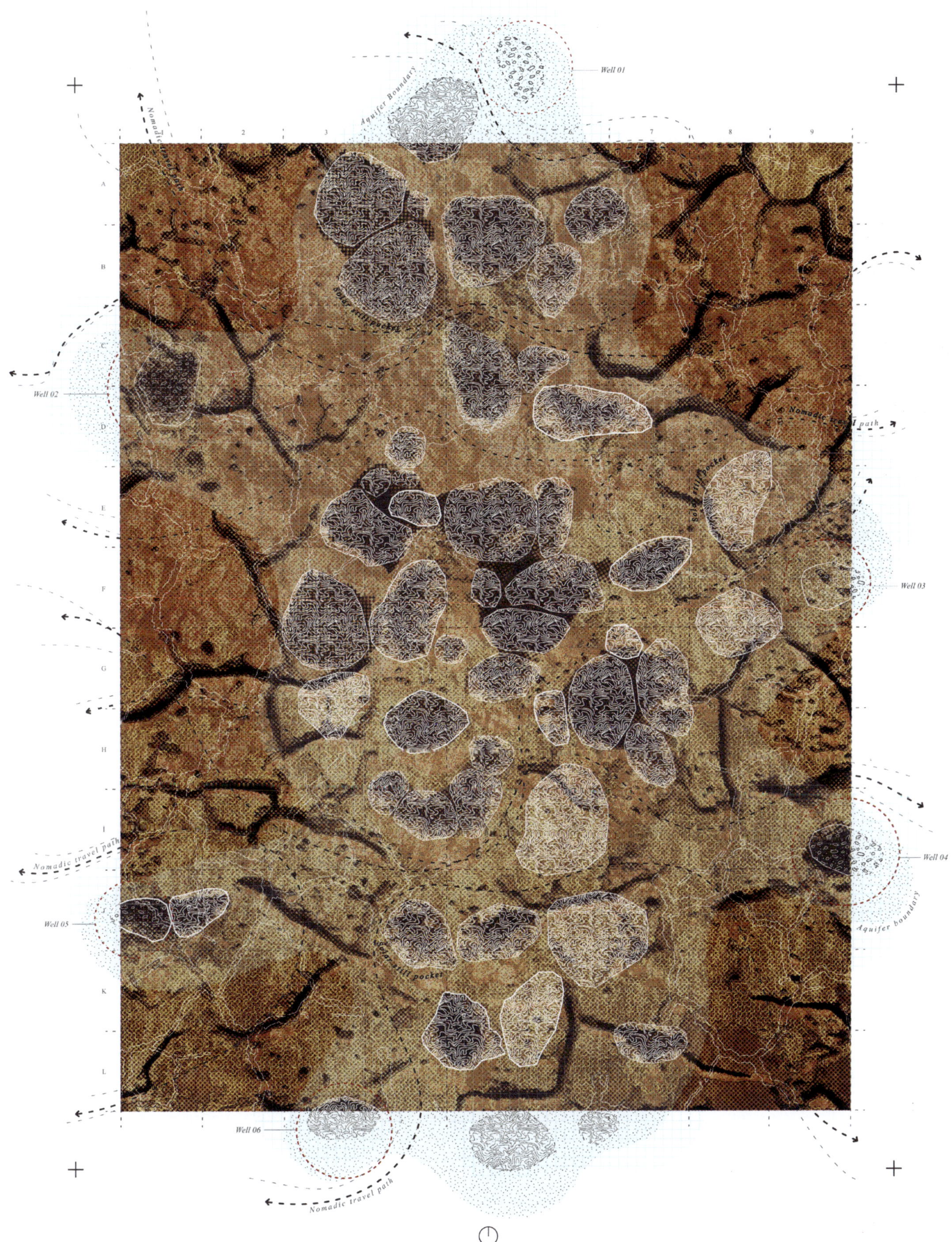

Well 01
Aquifer Boundary
Nomadic travel path
Well 02
Nomadic travel path
Well 03
Nomadic travel path
Well 04
Aquifer boundary
Well 05
Well 06
Nomadic travel path

UNEARTHING NARRATIVES IN THE LANDSCAPE

Nelson Byrd Woltz
Landscape Architects

Figure 01. Road through the citrus groves to Whakorekoretekai, the historic Māori cemetary. The strong central alignmnet of the bridge, road, and citrus *allée* serve as a ceremonial entrance to the burial mound.

Cultural, historical, and ecological narratives are not just critical to a fuller understanding of history; they lay the foundation for healing and future discourses on justice and humanism. They have the potential to reflect our values and how we choose to live and evolve with our environment. Intentional landscapes have the power to unearth, immerse, remind, and inspire. Moreso, it is possible for landscapes to reflect the democratic and egalitarian principles we strive for.

ORONGO STATION

Orongo Station, New Zealand, is a 1,200-hectare site consisting not only of a sheep station and working farm, but also an ecological reserve and an active Māori cemetery, called Whakorekoretekai. For the Ngāi Tāmanuhiri, a local Māori tribe, Whakorekoretekai is a sacred part of funereal rites. Their tradition is to have the *Tangihanga* (traditional Māori funeral rites) in the *marae* (open, cleared meeting space reserved for religious or social activities) in the nearby village of Muriwai, and then bring the body to the cemetery for the final service and interment. Around one to two years after the death, another ceremony is held to inaugurate a headstone or memorial marker.

Historically, the Ngāi Tāmanuhiri, who currently number around 1,200 people that primarily live in Muriwai, controlled the lands around Orongo Station. Physical traces of their historic settlements persist on the site in the form of earthworks, terracing, and excavations from food stores, huts, and defensive barriers of villages long past. These surviving archaeological remnants, etched into the face of the landscape, are protected under the jurisdiction of the New Zealand Historic Places Trust. Yet, the intersection between livestock and archaeology had deleterious effect, with the stamping of hooves into rain-saturated grounds causing irreparable damage to historic and sacred grounds.

This was an opportunity to harmonise ecology, culture, and history through landscape that honors each of these aspects. Our firm served as the bridge for dialog between the private landowner and the local Māori. Together, we designed a new site plan concept that purposefully locates programmatic zones, viewsheds, and circulation routes that pay homage to Whakorekoretekai. The site of potential cultural conflict - animal farming versus Māori history and sacred grounds - becomes a site of cross-cultural exchange and harmonious interaction: A new Ngāi Tāmanuhiri-run nursery provides plants for the vast reforestation efforts, and earthwork gardens honor iwi (Māori tribal) constructions.

MEMORIAL PARK

The historic Camp Logan, sited in the current Memorial Park in Houston, Texas and built in haste, was the temporary home and training grounds for nearly 30,000 men sent to train for combat in France during World War 1. Camp Logan was later deconstructed after the war's end. Traces of this training camp are sparse, spotted only in the concrete foundations of bathhouses and in the

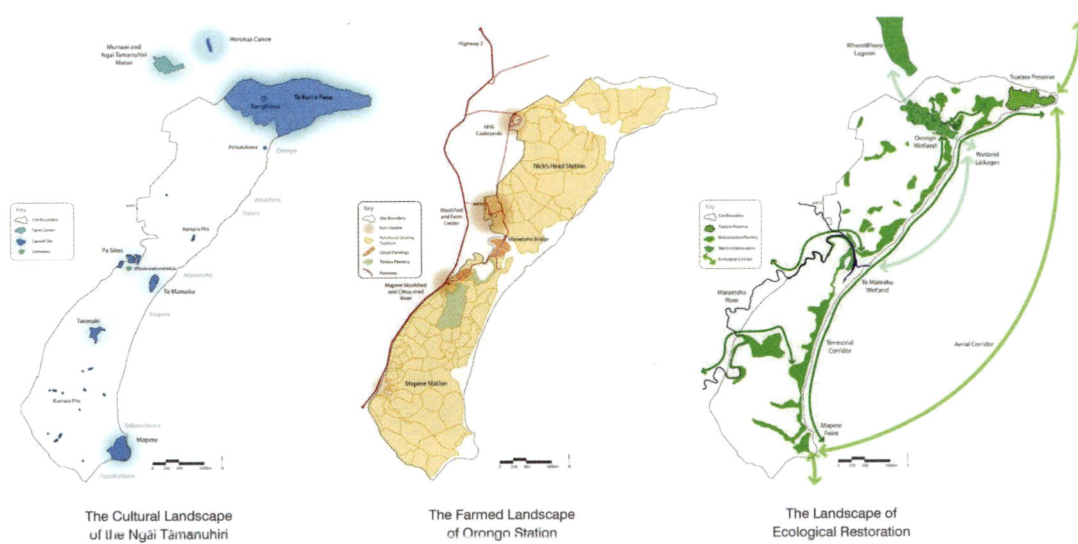

Figure 02. Cultural layers embeded in the local ecology.

traces of roads and other remnant foundations for structures with unknown purposes.

There is another storied quietly buried in Camp Logan: that of the 1917 Houston Riot. Black American soldiers served in the 370th Infantry Regiment and were stationed there during the racially violent Jim Crow era in America. They served alongside the 129th Infantry, 130th Infantry, and the machine gun battalions, earning commendations and medals from the French government for their valour, sacrifice, and service in the war. Their overseas commendation contrasted sharply with the hostility and abuse they experienced in their homeland.

Jim Crow laws and sensibilities were deeply embedded in the city of Houston. Businesses safely practiced segregation, while the white police force routinely harassed and provoked the black population in Houston - this included the black soldiers. They faced open and increasing hostility from the local white population, who were agitated at seeing blacks in military uniforms. Racial tensions escalated until an incident of police brutality broke the fragile peace. The ensuing riot resulted in twenty deaths, which included soldiers, policemen, and civilians. After a military court martial, nineteen black soldiers were hung onsite on scaffolding constructed from bathhouse timber. That the instruments of execution were once part of the toilets that these same medal-bearing soldiers had used, is a forgotten and bitterly ironic detail intimately intertwined with the larger narrative of Camp Logan.

The current Memorial Groves plan would transform ninety acres of Memorial Park into a living tribute to these soldiers and the larger regiment who lived and trained there from 1917-1918. In the proposed design, regimental rows of loblolly pines recall the thousands of individual soldiers, marching up to the native grassland savannah landscape in Memorial Park. To underscore the site's historical agency, we envision that Houston's various community members come together to harvest discrete groups of these trees for timber on a twenty-five-year cycle, a number that represents the average age of a soldier in the war. The milled timber might then be processed for use in public housing construction, suggesting the critical landscape's own sacrifice in service of the nation. The original seven Camp Logan-era roads will frame the park, with new bike and pedestrian paths that invite urban Houstonians to archaeological interpretation sites highlighted throughout the groves. The civic and monumental scale of the design proposal will play a pivotal role in reimagining the identity and culture of the city, communicating the sense of civic duty, sacrifice, and renewal that shape the stories of Memorial Park.

NBW would continue to engage school groups, veterans, and diverse community members in the place-making process for the old Camp Logan site. This approach is especially important given the issues of racism and police brutality that we are still facing today. As the project elements move from the monumental to intimate, the mutiny

Figure 03. Rendering of the imagined design for Memorial Groves, as-built.

of 1917 will be a special opportunity to foreground these issues in a public space. We want to ensure, from the very beginning of the design proces, that Memorial Groves strikes the right balance in addressing these complex, sensitive issues of discrimination, sacrifice, and civic duty.

ED JOHNSON MEMORIAL - LEARNING AND RECONCILIATION

In addition to memorialising, landscape can provide the platform for a transformative experience. The Ed Johnson Memorial in Chattanooga, Tennessee will relate the tragedy that resulted in a landmark court ruling which changed the very foundations of civil rights law in America.

It is said that there are three chapters in the Ed Johnson story: the lynching of Johnson, the courageous advocacy by two African-American attorneys, and the judicial precedent set forth by the case. Ed Johnson, a young black man in his twenties accused of raping a white woman in a trial devoid of incriminating facts, was sentenced to death by an all-white jury in 1906. Noah Parden and Styles Hutchins, two black attorneys, represented Johnson despite death threats; their homes were burned to the ground and they were forced to flee Chattanooga. They successfully made the case for a stay of Johnson's execution. Nevertheless, Johnson received 'trial by mob' and was dragged down to Walnut Street Bridge where a mob of whites beat, hung, and shot Johnson. His last words, later inscribed on his tombstone, were 'God bless you all. I AM a innocent man.' The case would go on to set as precedent the supremacy of Supreme Court oversight in civil rights cases, grant all defendants a right to a fair trial and effective counsel, and prohibit prejudicial juror selection.

In a sense, the historical lynchings have sadly transitioned to systemic lynchings. Institutionalised discrimination is among one of many unofficially sanctioned methods, and it is common knowledge that police brutality continues to this day. To foster contemporary conversation around these difficult topics, we proposed a 'Living Memorial' as the central design concept. The memorial plaza could house rotating works of art over the course of a year, such as sculpture, two-dimensional works, or performance pieces. Thus, local and national artists, in a nod to Chattanooga's own cultural heritage, would have the chance to employ lively creativity in reinterpreting Johnson's death and its significant legacy.

Community events would be planned on 19th March, the day of the lynching, and throughout the year to celebrate, mourn, and commemorate Ed Johnson and his legacy. No longer a static space, this living memorial would compel visitors to return to it and become part of its expression. In this way, the landscape might bear witness to the transformation of a violent mob from over 100 years ago into a present-day assembly of peaceful, introspective dialogue so necessary for the healing process. Only in this way can we hope to create a more just and equitable society.

Designing spaces that welcome all people diverse in culture, race, and ability is at the heart of our practice. Americans are currently witnessing memorials and public space being contested. Ever more diverse and buried narratives are being brought to light every day, and it is especially crucial to ground these stories in the landscape, creating places of memory that are real and present as we seek to confront hard truths about our past. We are honored to be a part of this awakening.

Figure 04. Conceptual rendering showing an example of the type of events planned for the 'living memorial'.

It is easy to be seduced by graceful curves, clever geometric forms, and lush foliage, but such landscapes can exhaust their lifespans relatively quickly unless seeded with meaningful intent that engages humanity and its history. The juxtaposition between the exquisite beauty of landscape and ugly historical horrors can be the catalyst for surprise, realisation, and eventually learning. The unfortunate aphorism – that those who do not learn history are doomed to repeat it – still stands true. The landscape provides opportunities to address some of the most painful and controversial moments of human history and engender healing and greater understanding, not just between people but also with the environment. It is the landscape, after all, that serves as the stage for our human dramas. It can also be the space where enrichment and progress occurs.

THE PATH FORWARD

Designing spaces that welcome all people diverse in culture, race, and ability is at the heart of our practice. Americans are currently witnessing memorials and public space being contested. Ever more diverse and buried narratives are being brought to light every day, and it is especially crucial to ground these stories in the landscape, creating places of memory that are real and present as we seek to confront hard truths about our past. We are honored to be a part of this awakening.

It is easy to be seduced by graceful curves, clever geometric forms, and lush foliage, but such landscapes can exhaust their lifespans relatively quickly unless seeded with meaningful intent that engages humanity and its history. The juxtaposition between the exquisite beauty of landscape and ugly historical horrors can be the catalyst for surprise, realization, and eventually learning. The unfortunate aphorism - that those who do not learn history are doomed to repeat it - still stands true. The landscape provides opportunities to address some of the most painful and controversial moments of human history and engender healing and greater understanding, not just between people but also with the environment. It is the landscape, after all, that serves as the stage for our human dramas. It can also be the space where enrichment and progress occurs.

THE CULTURAL INTERFACE

Jock Gilbert and Sophia Pearce

In this contested space between the two knowledge systems, the cultural interface (Nakata, 1998), things are not clearly black or white, Indigenous or Western. In this space are histories, politics, economics, multiple and interconnected discourses, social practices and knowledge technologies which condition how we all come to look at the world, how we come to know and understand our changing realties in the everyday, and how and what knowledge we operationalise in our daily lives. Much of what we bring to this is tacit and unspoken knowledge, those assumptions by which we make sense and meaning in our everyday world ... It is also important to understand what happens when Indigenous knowledge is documented in ways that disembodies it from the people who are its agents, when the "knowers" of that knowledge are separated out from what comes to be "the known", in ways that dislocates it from its locale, and separates it from the social institutions that uphold and reinforce its efficacy, and cleaves it from the practices that constantly renew its meanings in the here and now.

Dr Martin Nakata,
2007[1]

We acknowledge the Barkandji people as the traditional owners of the Country on and through which most of these insights have been gleaned, their Elders past, present and future.

We acknowledge the Culpra Milli Aboriginal Corporation (CMAC) whose generosity in sharing knowledge has made this possible.

Australia's Murray-Darling Basin presents an opportunity to envision what it might mean to begin to work at the "cultural interface". The territorial approach of government to the basin exemplifies the primacy of economics and privileges of global networks of capitalism, over the qualities and potentials of the land on which our regions, towns and cities are built.

A quintessentially "Australian" landscape, a quiet bucolic view, (Figure 1) shows the Murray River, taken from Culpra Station in New South Wales, looking towards Victoria. The water is low, reasonably clear and flows gently towards the ocean in South Australia.

But, this water is highly commodified - divided up, separated into "buckets" of high security water, low security water, environmental water, cultural water - most of which can be traded on national and global markets. And we're standing on an ancient Aboriginal fish trap - a remarkable piece of hydraulic engineering perhaps several thousand years old - and it's still a great place to catch fish. Up and down the river bank adjacent to this site are ancient middens evidencing networks of abundance, supporting generations across millennia.

Arguably, beginning to be evidenced here in this image are the spatialised ontological dualisms which Martin Nakata[2] understands as being 'so disparate as to be "incommensurable" on cosmological, epistemological and ontological grounds'. These constitute the cultural interface, and we are describing ways in which to work at this interface, to work productively through incommensurability rather than be caught in stultifying binaries.

1. Nakata, M 2007, 'The Cultural Interface', The Australian Journal Of Indigenous Education, vol. 36, Supplement.

2. Ibid. 1.

3. Murray Darling Basin Authority, Discover the Basin, viewed 3 December, 2018, <https://www.mdba.gov.au/discover-basin>

4. Bates, William 'Badger', When they take the water from a Barkandji person, they take our blood, The Guardian, accessed 3 December 2018, <https://www.theguardian.com/commentisfree/2017/jul/26/when-they-take-the-water-from-a-barkandji-person-they-take-our-blood>

5. Rose, D.B 1996, Nourishing Terrains: Australian Aboriginal views of landscape and wilderness, Australian Heritage Commission, pp.7.

Figure 01.
The Murray river, taken from Culpra station on NSW, looking towards Victoria.

The Murray-Darling Basin (MDB) is enormous. According to the Murray-Darling Basin Authority[3], it covers over a million square kilometres in south-eastern Australia, an area larger than the combined size of France and Germany. The MDB is home to over two million people and covers about forteen per cent of Australia's landmass These landscapes are home to at least thirty five endangered species of birds, sixteen endangered species of mammals and fourty six known species of native fish. It is Australia's most important agricultural region, producing around one third of the national food supply – it generates thirty nine per cent of the national income derived from agricultural production. It includes 77,000 kilometres of rivers and more than 25,000 wetlands (eleven of these are protected under the Ramsar Convention of Wetlands of International Importance). Of the approximately 13,000 gigalitres of flow in the basin, which studies have shown to be divertible, 11,500 gigalitres are removed for irrigation, industrial use and domestic supply. Agricultural irrigation accounts for about ninety five per cent of the water removed, including for the growing of rice and cotton.

In pursuit of the political dream to render marginal Mallee country productive, Alfred Deakin travelled to California and met George and William Benjamin Chaffey, the brothers who revolutionised the irrigation industry along the river Murray. In 1884, Alfred Deakin, the Victorian Minister for Public Works and Water Supply, was under considerable political pressure to develop a profitable irrigation industry in Victoria. As a result of this the desert did indeed bloom, with agricultural and horticultural industries thriving and supporting the development of communities and settlements throughout the region.

Issues of governance across state boundaries forced the establishment of the Murray-Darling Basin Authority and the implementation of the Murray-Darling Basin Plan, which was signed off by Tony Burke, Minister for Sustainability, Environment, Water, Population and Communities on 22 November 2012. The government interpretation is that the plan must give equal weight to the environmental, social, and economic impacts of irrigation. And so, we have agricultural operations running on global capital – including Cubbie Station whose water storages can be seen from space – allegedly competing with social and environmental water use.

Arguably this has resulted in a situation whereby the condition of the majestic Darling River in western NSW has been reduced to a pathetic dribble. Once an ephemeral system rising and falling, spreading water across a flood-plain up to eighty kilometres in width, the Darling is now largely a controlled minimal flow, confined to running well within the channel of it's "banks". The result of an ontological position through which water is separated and measured as a resource – the measurement is reduced to frameworks that render it impossible to look beyond the channel in which the water "normally" runs. The implications for communities along the river which rely physically and culturally on the river are disastrous.

Figure 02.
Knowledge exchange and sharing on Country at Culpra Station in a more formal setting.

Barkandji elder and Wilcannia man, Badger Bates, has written evocatively of this situation: 'When they take the water from a Barkandji person, they take our blood'.[4]

Badger's position eloquently set forward in a recent Guardian article, captures the spirit of an alternative ontological position whereby Country is conceived by Deborah Bird Rose as being:

'... a place that gives and receives life. Not just imagined or represented, it is lived in and lived with. Country is multi-dimensional...it consists of people, animals, plants, Dreamings, underground, earth, soils, minerals and waters, surface water, and air... Country has origins and a future; it exists both in and through time. Country, ideally, is synonymous with life.'[5]

For Barkandji people, the river (Baaka) is life itself.

Agricultural practices in the upper catchment have had a real and devastating impact on Aboriginal communities and Country along the Darling River and beyond. Recent revelations indicate that in 2016 irrigators at the top of the system were removing and stockpiling[6] water for their huge cotton farms, irrevocably damaging the health, wellbeing and cultural identity of Traditional Owners who have lived beside and through the River for millennia, in a mutually nourishing relationship.

The multi-dimensionality and entanglement inherent in the notion of Country and its mutually nourishing relationships is shared by the forty autonomous nations and 75,000 Indigenous people who live in the Murray-Lower Darling region alone. This affords an alternative mapping of the Basin and allows an introduction to the Barkandji people's story of the Darling River and its creation.

Considering the confluence of the Murray and Darling Rivers prompts the Ngatjinngulu Story as Sophia's Barkandji reading of Country:

> The Ngatjinngulu is the story of two Ngatjiis travelling and making our Country. Ngatjii is the Barkandji serpent of creation and nngulu means two in Barkandji language. One was Kuluwirru and the other was Watranyurinya who went north and Kuluwiiru travelled to Wirtiga (Mt Manara Kunjas Country), where the emu lost his wings, the stories of the crow ancestor (a major demigod in my Kunjas clan) and the two women, who eventually travel and make their own stories travelling and they end up as two pages in South Australia.

6. Chan, G 2017, 'Murray-Darling Basin: allegations of water theft spark calls for judicial inquiry' The Guardian, online, viewed 3 December 2018 <https://www.theguardian.com/australia-news/2017/jul/25/murray-darling-basin-allegations-of-water-theft-spark-calls-for-judicial-inquiry>

7. McGaw & Pieris 2015, Assembling the Centre: Architecture for Indigenous Cultures - Australia and beyond, Abington, Oxon, Routledge.

8. Pearce, S 2013, Kanyita's Way: A Reflection on Yarning, unpublished Master's thesis, Charles Sturt University.

9. McGaw & Pieris 2015, Assembling the Centre: Architecture for Indigenous Cultures - Australia and Beyond, Routledge, Abington, Oxon.

10. Ibid. 9.

11. Pearce, Barry. Personal communication - many, on Country.

12. Ibid. 10.

Figure 03.
Knowledge exchange and sharing on Country at Culpra Station in a more informal setting.

Ngatjinngulu Parrintji created the Kirree Kira and in their travels they created the waterholes and trees - our food - guarded by deities and rituals, enabling our old people and ancestors to recognise us. So they named these places in our language.

When Ngatjinngulu met underground they mated - the result of giant serpents' mating is the body fluids create the wet marshes and underground soakage points, hence the sacredness of these stories can often belong to men. The language with mating describes our body parts and their relationship to all living things.

The opals of the White Cliffs region are the result of the Ngatjis gurna (faeces) as if the amazing rainbow serpent would have anything other than precious minerals as excrement.

These stories of Country (territory) explain our cultural responsibility to care and protect all of our sacred places.

The architects Janet McGaw and Anoma Pieris quote Marcia Langton in describing "Story" as a 'spiritual power that is ubiquitous in particular persons and places... an essence that is immutable'[7] and which is enmeshed within the concept of Country through a living relationship. '"To be" is to know one's Story and to enact it on Country'.

In this methodology, story-telling is enabled through "yarning", an approach that through the work of Sophia Pearce[8], affords each party the opportunity to locate themselves in the story of the other. Storying (through the vehicle of the yarn) requires attention to "deep listening". McGaw and Pieris[9] quote Brearley and Hamm, in describing deep listening as beginning with 'sharing stories and offering an opportunity for each party to situate themselves in the story of the other. It is a process that takes time and requires patience.' They go on to quote Egyptian scholar Samia Mehrez who similarly argues that 'it is only when the coloniser accepts their place in the narrative of dispossession that the work of decolonisation can begin'.[10]

In doing so, each party is also then situated in and on Country. The understanding of Country is dependent on the unfurling of the understanding of one's part in it and can only be gained in relation to the parts of others engaged through the yarn. It is a process that takes time and requires patience, as well as an inclination to listening deeply. It is a process in which knowledge is often shared during everyday practices - sharing a meal, cup of tea, around a campfire. The yarn depends upon an openness towards the chance encounter as much as on the "organised".

Aboriginal representation in management and regulation with the MDB is increasing through bodies including: Murray Lower Darling Rivers Indigenous Nations (MLDRIN), Living Murray Indigenous Partnerships Projects (LMIPP) and Aboriginal Waterways Assessment Program (AWA).

However, the way these initiatives are undertaken is critical to their success - and we think that the notion of Country, it's entanglements, it's relationship to Story, the yarn and the necessity to engage in "deep listening", provides a means through which landscape architects and the design professions might contribute to this.

Demonstrating this are some images of a workshop - Interpretive Wonderings - in which the authors collaborated, along with Campbell Drake from University of Technology Sydney and Sven Mehzoud of Monash University with CMAC - knowledge is unfurled on Country through a shared concern - the allowance of space for the yarn formally (Figure 2) as well as (Figure 3) informally.

Figure 04.
Spring regeneration at Culpra Station.

Knowledge exchange and sharing, underpinned by deep listening, is more likely to happen in the allowance of these informal "interstitial" moments - where day to day "stuff" is happening.

This is spring regeneration on Culpra Station (Figure 04). It's the result of the long slow wetting (sometimes called a flood) that occurred at the end of the "big dry" of the early 2000s. Many of the Black Box (Eucalyptus largiflorens) in the background have succumbed to the extended dry but most are regenerating now. The daisies and other herbs have replenished beautifully.

Describing the way water moves through country, (Figure 05) points to an inherent difficulty in the thinking of water as buckets (resource). An environmental flow is managed and delivered - often quickly. It frequently happens, independent of broader river recharge events. Its fast delivery precludes the long slow soaking of a natural event. In this image, two things are happening (they're related, and they consequently lead to the flourishing evident in the previous image): the water is moving very slowly through the landscape - it penetrates and soaks, wetting the soil profile. More remarkably this is water moving through Country, uphill against the gradient, a remarkable observation of Barry and Betty Pearce, the Mutthi Mutthi and Barkindji elders respectively - caretakers and custodians of the lands within Culpra Station. Pressure from the river flow forces water slowly back up the billabongs and flood runners long after the rain has stopped, and overland flow diminished. This is a paradox described by Barry as - 'all water is wet'![11]

So, Country requires people, people to be listening deeply - to each other, to and through the land (scape). To quote Uncle Barry Pearce - 'brother, we may think we own the land, but the land owns us'.[12] It behoves us as landscape architects to listen.

Figure 05.
Water moving through Country.

IN CONVERSATION

Charles Massy

THE CALL OF THE REED WARBLER

Image by KERB

The following are a selection of ideas from a round-table conversation with Charles Massy, author of Call of the Reed Warbler: A New Agriculture - A New Earth, in May 2018. Massy is a farmer developing regenerative agriculture practices in New South Wales' Monaro region, as well as a research associate at the Fenner School of Environment and Society at the Australian National University. The invitational discussion was organised between students of the RMIT Landscape Architecture program and senior lecturer Jock Gilbert and brought together land managers, designers, educators and agriculturalists. The informal session spanned topics from Indigenous land management to fertiliser, firestick farming and urban irrigation.

Paul Appleton, Associate Landscape Architect, Nelson Byrd Woltz: You made a note of fire practice and the use of fire in land management and gave the indication that this knowledge is still alive and that tradition is unbroken. I was wondering firstly how intact that is across the whole country? Are there people who can teach what they know? And also a side question: if there are gaps, how applicable is the knowledge from one region to another? And how site specific is that experience?

Charles Massy: It's a good question to start with. I'd say first that I'm no world expert. I've been a generalist talking to others - people like Bill Gammage.

And even though it was a big book, we took a lot out. One of those stories was a trip up to the Daly River country in the Top End. As some of you might be aware ... it's one of the richest environmental groups in the world and land managers up there are brilliant at doing counterintuitive things. They've bought big licks of Country in Cape York, the Top End and the Kimberley and then handed them over to the Indigenous Land Corporation. Fish River is an old cattle station... it's pretty remote with some unique, difficult country. There were something like thirty endangered species in it, it was that rich. They then worked with some of the leading scientists, who were looking at the carbon issues and emissions.

What has resulted is that it has brought some of the Elders, who have switched from hot season burning with a huge release of nitrous oxide and carbon dioxide, to traditional cool season burning. They've reduced emissions by eighty-five percent, and they've now got major carbon credit income lined up with QANTAS and people like that. Suddenly you've got the Elders involved. So to answer your question, in that area, the skills are still with the remaining Elders. But across lots of Australia, they're not. You've got a lot of Indigenous young generation who are desperately looking to regain the skills. And that guy I showed you last night - the elder back home - he's busy teaching from Tasmania up to Sydney, park rangers and things.

The beauty of Rod Mason - the guy I showed in the lecture - is that on his mother's side he's Pitjantjatjara, so he grew up and only had to burn spinifex, as well as knowing our Country's invasive grasslands. There's not a lot like him. He knows that as a regenerative tool, there's about ten or twelve compounds in smoke that have a stimulatory impact on propagating seed, let alone the heat factors. I think it's a really important space, that for all sorts of reasons hasn't been examined. Shape mosaic burnings ... when do you do it, what time of day? There's some amazing correlations if you get the burning right in the autumn when you have a much cooler burn, you get longer lasting bio-char carbon. It's a whole space that hasn't been opened up.

Phillipa Murray, Lecturer, Interior Design, RMIT: Just talking about soils... so my dad is an old school farmer. It's interesting reading your book about Australian soils being ancient and not responsive to some European farming techniques. If you spoke to my dad, he'd be adamant you'd have to add phosphorus or nitrogen, and I understand that over time these are not the right process. Are there any cases of regenerating soil health if you use fertiliser?

Charles Massy: The Western two thirds of Australia, which is known as the Western Shield, is what's really ancient. A lot of the Eastern third is volcanic and more recent material so it's not so simple. At home, for example, our basalts are about 40 million, going onto about 440 million years old, with our metamorphic rocks going to about half a billion.

If you want to regenerate, which is what's happening in grazing, once you get your groundcover up, you get animal impacts. I alluded to yesterday the self organising capacities found in American prairies and rangelands. Once you get your soils working, seeds that have been buried for over a hundred years are being brought up by bugs, and suddenly we have found three or four new grasses at home, never seen before.

That's an example of pragmatic self-organisation. Now if you go into an Australian grassland and put on a heavy dusting of super-phosphates, it's like a poison to a lot of our natives. That's a sort of purist view. In environments that are heavily modified by the plow, farmers have got to survive with increased production. It's easy for me to say "no fertiliser" but in the interim farmers have to stay viable. But speaking to Western Australian croppers, the evidence is mounting in the big-cropping science that nitrogenous fertilisers, which come from fossil fuels, are making the cereals a lot more vulnerable to frosts - so declining yields, against high costs.

So the system's starting to hit a wall from what I've seen in the broad-cropping areas, and that's without factoring in what those heavy doses of fertilisers are doing to the microorganisms, that now aren't sourcing the nutrients!

How do you answer that question? You say go turn off the tap, and you get a lot of farmers going to the wall. It's a difficult one.

Fiona Harrison, Lecturer, Landscape Architecture, RMIT: On water and the urban landscape, it's a direct correlation through how we deal with irrigation and the earth. When we're building a park, do we think of that piece of earth we are working with as an ecological system? And if we think about a living system, it holds more water and is more durable in drought. We deal with earth and we move earth but do we really manage it as an ecological system in relation to irrigation?

We have a mechanical mind in many ways, when we water things; it is similar to that mechanical mind rather than thinking of it as a living, holding system.

Claire Martin, Associate Director, OCULUS: A lot of what we do as landscape architects, is to try and minimise the reliance on potable water and irrigation. But even the use of irrigation as a contrived use of water, to generate particular landscapes, can change the perception of those and even if it's as much as putting plants that are not meant to be in that place and not meant to look that way. That is not to say that we shouldn't do it but to understand the implications to broader hydrological resource systems and understanding how it can be offset and what the benefits are.

Charles Massy: It's interesting, right? At the end of the book I threw in some ideas which are a bit fluid – I see these leading regenerative farmers with modern scientific, ecological knowledge. I would regard them as having moved to a third mind, which I've called the emergent mind. Combining the best of science with the best of the organic, which shouldn't be static but should be evolving in a self-organising way. It means combining the best of the fields. I think the best regenerative practitioners that I've met are almost identical to Rod and his compatriots… and that's what's best for Country. And that's a totally different worldview. If you then combine that with some really good ecological and soil science and that's the sort of new space it's being moved into. That's just another spin on some of the spiritual issues, something to chew on; I could be quite wrong. There's certainly a different mind now in operations that's not just ancient Indigenous knowledge but scientific as well. And what are the pitfalls of each?

I was speaking to Aunty Ruby, an elder from Brisbane. We were talking about spirituality and her connection to Country and she actually brought in her connection to water. Often when we see Country, we see it as the hard landscapes and not the fluid with the life force it brings with it. Her connection to the water is for it to be celebrated in every form. That it is utilised and we can utilise it. Understanding there is actually a connection; a spirituality to water and the movement and life force it has. Understanding how that can form in our urban landscapes, and in rural as well. If we are able to somehow understand that connection with the fluid, then what can that mean in our own practices?

Rosie, Graduate of Landscape Architecture: I wonder if that is linked to the spaces that we inhabit as practitioners. If we're talking about an individualised engagement with country and landscape, my experience as being a student in this building was one that is very, very disconnected from the landscape. Since leaving RMIT I've started things like composting, growing vegetables in my garden, speaking to my neighbours and I feel much more connected to the landscape. I wonder how each of us individually connects to the landscape currently in our own lives and how that relates to the questions we're talking about.

Charles Massy: I'm just wondering whether you guys don't carry the baggage that we have created through 200 years of the mechanical mind belting the landscape. You're coming with a whole different worldview and you could be leading this shift to a better ecological mind.

Riley Donaldson, Design Consultant, Nelson Byrd Woltz: In Australian landscape architecture there's been anxiety about the natural and not wanting to touch the natural, and perhaps it's our cultural ideas about the natural, but writers like yourself and Bill Gammage are shifting that idea of what that natural landscape might be. The perception is moving towards something that was curated and isn't as natural as we picture it.

A SHARED DESIGN METHOD WHICH BETTER INTEGRATES COMMUNITIES

Annacaterina Piras

It is not possible to talk about the city without thinking of the people who compose it, and it is not possible to talk about the resilience of the urban landscape without looking at social inclusion. Nowadays our cultural landscapes present themselves not only as the stratification of a sophisticated socio-ecological mosaic that has overlapped over time, but also the result of a vortex of flows of people, goods and services; one that leaves a multitude of signs. Signs which are open, more than ever, to multiple interpretations.

Within the disciplinary framework of landscape architecture, we are witnessing a flourishing and proliferation of participatory urban practices. Naturally this puts increased pressure on the already urgent and spasmodic search for answers around how to go about community-based construction of places of meaning. We believe finding these answers will be an essential step for landscape architecture as it continues to work to pinpoint exactly what role it has to play as a discipline in the production of space in the city.

As such, in 2016 we established the LandWorks Circus International Program (www.lwcircus.org), a program with the main research intention of engaging with the city in a way that pushes the boundaries of landscape architecture into the realms of cultural landscapes in both urban and rural contexts.

Based on a narrative of a sort of renaissance within the urban landscape, LWCircus's research centres around the engagement programs of the ArnoLabs shared creative workshops. In particular, we are working on experimentation through artistic and multimedia languages, which through the medium of art in the landscape can give back meaning to places and reconstruct ways of living in, and enhancing, the landscape. This is something that we believe emerges most strongly when communities actively contribute to the construction of their cities, as it happened in the past during the renaissance period.

As such, our work is deliberately based on a necessarily participatory formula that enables local communities to work cooperatively in urban landscapes and prestigious environments to share and build places of exchange and interaction. This is a process that moves disparate communities towards social inclusion, giving rise to ephemeral installations

1. Mastinu, M & Saiu, V 2016, Ricerche di Architettura e di Urbanistica, Una rassegna di tesi di dottorato, Publica, Alghero.

2. Bussiere, S & Lovell, K 2016, 'Design and Experiential Learning in Post-Industrial Landscapes', Landscape Research Record No. 5.

3. Piras, A, 2016, 'LandWorks Workshop, a fruitful way to re-evaluate cultural landscapes', Landuum, Paisaje, Cultura y Diseno, no. 2.

4. Piras, A 2018, 'SPECIAL - LA RIVOLUZIONE VERDE DELLA CITTA' by Loredana Barillaro, Magazine di arte contemporanea, vol. VII, no. 25.

5. Piras, A 2018 'LWCircus Shared Operative Program, Landscape Design Methods based on Social Practices for an Inclusive and Resilient Urban Future', IFLA World Congress Singapore, Future Resilience, July 2018.

6. Piras, A, Camarena, P and Porraz, M 2018, 'LWCircus ArnoLab 2018: integración social y resiliencia a través el paisaje', Landuum, Paisaje y Resiliencia, no. 09.

that sit somewhere between art and landscape; perhaps what we can define as a sort of urban land art.

The protagonists of this project are of course the places and people who interact with it in various ways. Local communities, minorities including political refugees and asylum seekers, administrators who are solicited by a multidisciplinary and an international creative community. All of these groups, through the use of artistic and multimedia languages, work cooperatively through our programs to revisit the historical memory of the places concerned and move towards a plausible future which is increasingly resilient and inclusive.

Focused on experimental methods and strategies of design based largely on social and cultural practices in the field, the LWCircus program aims to explore sensitive areas around cultural heritage and redesigning contemporary urban landscapes which are currently undergoing environmental, social and economic transition.

LWCircus looks for alternative tools to activate sustainable development and responsible action through shared workshops, the direct involvement of local communities, minorities and well-known international practitioners. The workshops stimulate the interdisciplinary exchange of knowledge, information, attitudes, skills and real-world know how through artistic and multi-media expression. The LWCircus program's outcomes aim towards an integration, and cultural and economic development whereby local inhabitants and minorities can feel connected and intertwined.

The first two editions of the shared operative workshops, (called LWCircus-ArnoLabs) were held in Florence. The first was over a ten-day period in September 2017, and the second over a similar period in May 2018. At these events a culturally and disciplinary disparate group of participants worked together to create ephemeral installations such as lighting solutions, urban furniture, staging points and temporary shelters. These were all realised on site through the collection and appropriation of recycled natural material transported to site by the unpredictable and changing fluctuations of the Arno river.

During both the events a temporary international, multi-cultural and multidisciplinary creative community emerged to fruitfully test shared practices by using multimedia languages, artistic approaches and performative/ spontaneous attitudes. This included the direct involvement of local actors and public institutions responsible for the river's safeguarding and management. All the groups involved in the workshop were looking for a "resilient" and "inclusive" urban future, and it was felt that they went a long way towards achieving responsible cultural valorisation and sustainable development for the local community, and the diverse minorities directly involved in each step of the process.

At both events, groups of selected young refugees, from Niger, Senegal, Mali (ArnoLab017), Burkina Faso, Ghana, Gambia and Bangladesh (ArnoLab018), who had survived the dangerous crossing of the Mediterranean, were invited to join the rest of the international creative group (from Mexico, China, USA, Australia, Lebanon and Syria, Colombia, Venezuela UK, Holland, France, and Italy). Everyone worked together extremely enthusiastically to design and realise the series of installations, sharing wishes and hopes, and kick-starting a process of social inclusion that gave life to successive opportunities for further entanglement of local realities.

By sharing the process in conceiving and realising the works, these disparate groups transmuted what started as the concept of "others" into a feeling of "us". The outcome we hoped for was a re-appropriation of traditional strategies for living along the riverbanks, where, through interaction, different members of the community could take over ownership and management of the reconquered public space without any kind of discrimination.

We believe that these results demonstrate a huge amount of potential around the evolution of the traditional figure of the landscape architect, to a sort of 'landscape facilitator' whose role is also to underline the operative shared method as a fundamental and intrinsic part of the design process. Making disparate groups feel as though they play a central part in achieving a result is essential for getting excellent results in a short time.

In the future it is hoped that this project will help to heal the landscapes together with their communities. This is a project that stimulates not just a sense of responsibility to landscape and place, but also to community. When landscapes are a product of community the two become inseparable, and when temporary or new arrival communities such as refugees or immigrants become engaged in these processes they become equally responsible for the production both of concrete and symbolic space, therefore they start to become equally embedded into local communities.

7. Piras, A 2018, 'Experimental shared practices strategies for Urban Renovation and Cultural Heritage valorization', The 7th International landscape planning and design Conference, WORLD HABITAT Magazine no. 05, Speech, pp. 20 & 21.

8. Piras, A 2018, 'LWCircus Shared Operative Program, Metodo di Progettazione basato sull'utilizzo di Pratiche Sociali Strategie sperimentali attraverso approcci partecipativi, linguaggi artistici e attitudini performative per il Rinnovamento del Paesaggio Urbano, la Valorizzazione dei Patrimoni Culturali e l'Inclusione Sociale nello Spazio Pubblico', Città Come Cultura, MAXXI Museum Foundation, Rome.

IN ORDER TO LISTEN: DISCOVERING AND RECOVERING LAND LITERACY

Stephanie Murray

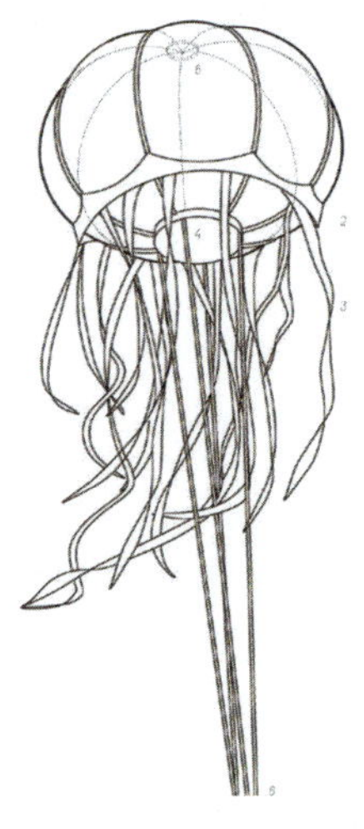

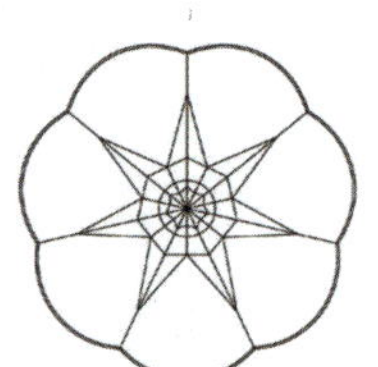

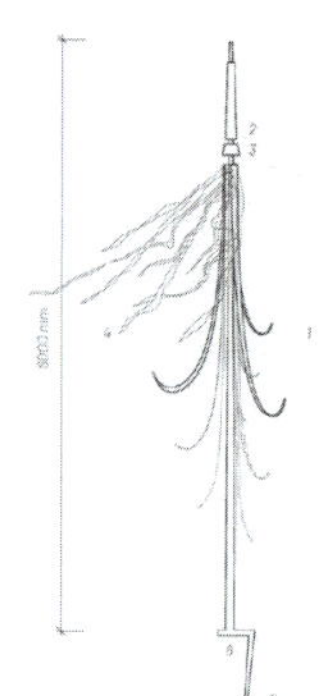

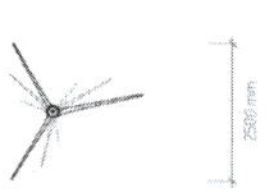

lit-er-acy
/'lideres, 'litres /noun

1. Competency or knowledge in a specified area,
2. A person's knowledge of a particular subject or field,
3. The ability to interpret, analyse, articulate and communicate indicators, signs and symbols within a specific system or ecological context.

Due to increased sedentation and settlement forced upon a people, their relationship with the land began to change. Over generations the intimate knowledge of a landscape would fade and patterns of the land would soon change, too.

After a time, the air moved differently and the soils were ever pushed as layers of earth were sculpted towards industrial goals. Water whispered frequent farewells and left dusty voids to tease the wind. The people who had roamed the land for centuries were fragmented by Israeli state development, segregating their expansive reach and corroding a delicate agreement with the unforgiving landscape that had defined their conditions of survival and vitality.

Collectively, the effects of the Anthropocene and climate change combine to create a land that is changing faster than methods of traditional Bedouin knowledge can accommodate. This is further emphasised by their forced sedentation and displacement - asserting a lifestyle that is less based on intimate land engagement and more on boldly forced political ideals of ambitious state advancement. In response to this, a network of instruments are situated across the landscape creating a readable system that is delicate and inevitably obsolescent. The instruments' response to the elements, paired with the memories of old wisdom, can be used to read the conditions and act as tools of navigation and survival on a land returned to the people. Positioned in a sublime and imaginary future on the Negev Desert, at the edge of agricultural endeavours and the terrain falling into the drainage basin; these instruments are resources informing a legibility of survival toward the discovery and recovery of land literacy.

Heat inflated balloons lift thin, delicate sheets of fabric as the air inside them is heated by the intense sun, rising.

Each "ghost tent" is located at the site of a well with an attached buoy, acting as a beacon to the water resource and a remembrance of a historic lifestyle.

The form of the fabric changes depending on temperature and water level in the well. A hygrometer senses the relative humidity through the movement of veneer strips of tamarisk: a local tree that has been historically used to indicate water presence by the Bedouin. The instrument indicates rain and the potential of flash floods in wadis. Piezoelectric wind ribbons power a light during storms. Hygrometer activation signals the placement of check dams which allow water to seep deeper through the surface, replenishing aquifers before the precious resource mixes into the undrinkable Dead Sea.

This change in groundwater becomes legible as it affects ghost tent formations.

LEFTUNDER
OFFICE

Not often a single project offer the chance for the reunification of a community, let alone twelve suburbs. A train line that has divided eight kilometres of suburban Melbourne into two for over 100 years is being elevated. This has created an opportunity for either side, which have developed independently to finally come together below, with enormous potential for civic, social and cultural repair. The train line, which first contributed to the growth of these communities, is now the very thing restricting them. What leftunder interrogates is how the momentum from a large infrastructural project can be opportunistically used to address a broad range of local issues. The 225,000m^2 of space created below the train line is simply a by-product of the Victorian Government's election promise to remove fifty of the most dangerous level crossings within Melbourne, and was never the intention of this undertaking. OFFICE saw that without the appropriate consultation and activism from the local community a half-hearted treatment of the space would be the result. It could be argued that the realised proposal is just that.

Questioning the traditional tools of the architect, leftunder became an independent online forum that assumed the role of facilitator in the engagement of these communities. The online forum allowed for new interactions between all those who have a stake in the project and traditionally tend not to be heard. To coordinate a series of projects below the extent of the eight kilometres train line, demands the need to facilitate and engage with a number of stakeholders. Traditionally the local residents are missing from this engagement, or are engaged with when it is too late. The leftunder website was our way of navigating and cataloguing the desires of these parties, as an open dialogue was established. By engaging with the local residents, leftunder directly addressed the complex social, economic and political make-up of the suburbs that the train line passes through allowing for site-specific responses. Establishing strong relationships within local residents and community groups, opportunities for the growth and occupation of these spaces arise, well past the completion of the infrastructure project.

An example of this process is the work OFFICE has done with AMES (Adult Multicultural Education Services) Noble Park who lease a plot of land adjacent to the rail corridor and wanted to explore the opportunity that they have in occupying the space below. Working closely with the regional manager we explored the skills and desires of the refugees and recent migrants in the area in creating a master plan that responds to their needs. By understanding the refugees' skill set unrecognised by the Australian government, the engagement highlighted the social and political issues present within this community, and the opportunity to identify these through the infrastructural project.

As a critique on current development leftunder is a model for a replicable platform, a project that addresses the lack of engagement within local communities affected by development. The project attempts to repair not only a spatial fissure, but hopes to repair the relationship between the general public and built environment professionals. As an independent group it's questionable how much impact it has had on the final design for the space below the line. The Victorian State Government released the final concept plans for the 225,000m^2 of linear park in early 2018, which appear to be a rollout of generic and hackneyed ideas. Late 2018 saw the next state election, timed perfectly with the completion of this infrastructural project. If we look past the freshly rolled turf, playgrounds and barbeques, will these spaces really help the local communities or will they see this as another misrepresentation and understanding of what is really needed?

TAX AGENT
SURUR AFRICAN SUPERMARK
NOBLE PARK

INSANE

GAUTHAM SARANG
Gautham Sarang grew up in Attappady, Palakkad, Kerala, on the Western Ghats. His parents believe that education is the practice of life. They selected a dying out, barren watershed for building their dream of a rural university. They wanted to find solutions for water scarcity, soil erosion, environmental destruction and so on. They protected the watershed which resulted in nature regenerating a small patch of forest along with a small water source. With some simple techniques, they regenerated the soil too. Gautham grew up amidst these regeneration activities.

Gautham's education was about 'taking' for his existence and 'leaving' for others' existence. Natural farming, cooking, building mud check dams, making traditional huts, knowing more about plants and animals, learning local technology, health, etc. were part of his life and education. Sarang is the name of the alternative school that his parents started (The rural university still remains a dream).

TAYLOR MILLER
Taylor Miller completed her BFA and MA in Art & Visual Culture Education at the University of Arizona. As a PhD student, her research interests include the contemporary cultural and political geography of Palestine, and the aesthetics and critical spatial practices of the Israeli occupation. Her transdisciplinary projects incorporate photography, poetry and critical architectural and urban theory. To view her work or contact, visit www.taylorkmiller.com

REVATHI SEKHAR KAMATH
Revathi Kamath was born in Bhubaneshwar, Orissa, in 1955. She obtained her Bachelors degree in Architecture in 1977 and a Post Graduate degree in Urban and Regional Planning in 1981, both from the Sch ool of Planning and Architecture, Delhi.

Kamath has gone on to become one of India's most highly regarded architects, and currently works as Principal Architect at Kamath Design.

GARETH POWELL
Gareth Powell is a *Wadawurrung* man, a former Director of the *Wadawurrung* (Wathaurung Aboriginal Corporation), and Director of LLB (Legals Lawyers Barristers) Ltd based in Canberra on *Ngunnawal* registration, Gareth has a keen interest in Native Title legal issues generally as it pertains to Australian Aboriginal communities, but also the *Wadawurrung* people specifically.

DAVID S JONES
David S Jones is Foundation Professor of Planning & Landscape Architecture at Deakin University, in Geelong, on *Wadawurrung* Country. He has a long-standing close working teaching, listening, and research relationship with the *Wadawurrung, Kaurna, Gunditjmara* and *Boon Wurrung* communities in landscape architecture and land planning topics aligned towards the scope of Country.

GARETH POWELL & DAVID S JONES
The article is part of their collective partnership of respectfully exploring and discussing legal issues relevant to *Wadawurrung* Country to better explain the complexities of what the *Wadawurrung* understand as their Country, and how this understanding is positioned within both *Wadawurrung* and Western legal contexts.

ÉMÉLIE DESROCHERS-TURGEON
Educated in Fine Arts, Émélie Desrochers-Turgeon began her doctoral studies in architecture at the Azrieli School of Architecture and Urbanism in 2017. She completed a bachelor's degree in Environmental Design at Université du Québec à Montréal and a Masters degree in Architecture at McGill University. Thanks to a grant from the Order of Architects of Quebec, she documented cultural landscapes in the community of Kangirtugaapik on Baffin Island, Nunavut. She has worked in Montreal and in Berlin on various architectural projects, as well as industrial design and exhibition design. Her projects and written works examine the issues of settler colonialism, landscape representation and architectural imagination. She is interested in how Western ideas about time and space are encoded in language, philosophy and architectural imagination. Her research looks into the notions of cross-cultural interpretation and deconstructing the colonial imagination that pertains to space.

WINTER COUNT
WINTERCOUNT is a union of artists cultivating awareness and fostering healing and protection for land and water, for all living things passed, and for all living things to come. The growing collective of multidisciplinary artists work in film, performance, installation, sculpture, storytelling and sound composition, engaging with landscapes under current threat by extractive industry. These conversations are ongoing, for everyone, and are accessible to the public through online platforms, museum and gallery exhibitions, screenings and public performances.

FIRESTICKS
Firesticks is an Indigenous led network and aims to re-invigorate the use of cultural burning by facilitating cultural learning pathways to fire and land management. It is an initiative for Indigenous and non- Indigenous people to look after Country, share their experiences and collectively explore ways to achieve their goals.

SCOTT RANKIN
Scott Rankin (born 1959 in Sydney) is an Australian theatre director, writer and co-founder and Creative Director of the arts and social change company Big hART. He works in and with isolated communities and diverse cultural settings, as well as in commercial performance.

MARIA GABRIELLA TROVATO
Maria Gabriella Trovato is Assistant Professor in the LDEM Department at the American University of Beirut. She gained a Phd in 2003 at the University of Reggio Calabria and the University of Naples in Landscape Architecture: Parks, Gardens and Spatial Planning.

ROBYN SMITH
Robyn Smith is a PhD (Political History), Master of Cultural Heritage and BA (Anthropology and Journalism). She is a history and heritage practitioner based in Darwin and has been involved in historical research and interpretation advice in respect of a range of sites. Smith has researched a number of Northern Territory massacres and intends to continue researching others.

JULIA WATSON
Julia Watson is the Founding Director of Studio Rede, a professor at Columbia University, a critic at Rhode Island School of Design, an expert at the Center for Resilient Cities and Landscapes and a New York State Council of the Arts Architecture + Design Independent Project judge. She is currently working on her first independent publication titled 'Ancient Innovations: From the Fourth to the First World', which received a New York State Council of the Arts grant, and is fiscally sponsored by Storefront for Art and Architecture. Julia is co-author of a spiritual guidebook titled, 'Guide to Bali's UNESCO World Heritage'.

PIERRE BÉLANGER
Dr. Pierre Bélanger is Associate Professor of Landscape Architecture at Harvard University's Graduate School of Design and Founding Director of Landscape Infrastructure Lab. Dr. Bélanger takes particular interest in the intersection of territory, ecology, and power. and is the recipient of the Professional Prix de Rome in Architecture award, Special Advisor to the US Army Corps of Engineers and Curator for the 2016 Canada Pavilion at the 2016 Venice Architecture Biennale.

KATE YOON

Kate Yoon is an independent writer, research assistant, and college student at Harvard University. She is a Canada Program Undergraduate Research Fellow and Associate at the Weatherhead Center for International Affairs at Harvard. Her research focuses on Immanuel Kant, cosmopolitanism, and Canadian migrants as political agents.

JULIETTE ANICH

Dr Juliette Anich is an active entrepreneur and researcher. Her interests lie in exploring environmental and social change through research, teaching and project development. Juliette has a Bachelor of Design from UNSW, a Masters in Business from RMIT where her thesis looked into ethical consumer behaviour and decision making. She went on to receive a scholarship for her PhD at RMIT, in the School of Architecture and Design, which explored environmental behaviours and activism in urban agricutlutre which was complete in August 2016.

LOUIS MITCHELL

Louis Mitchell is a freelance cinematographer and photographer, currently based in Melbourne, Australia. His focus in both art practices is largely independent documentary work. Louis' work has been exhibited and published locally and internationally. Louis' years of work in the camera departments of Australian television have always helped to fund his next independent photo or video project. Louis enjoys the freedom of shifting from the solo focus of his photography projects to working as part of a team with other creatives to realise a vision for film.

DARCY RANKIN

Darcy Rankin is a settler who grew up on Tommeginner Country in NW Tasmania. He is a current candidate for the Masters of Landscape Architecture at RMIT. Darcy's research is concerned with the Onto-pathological condition of Settler Australia and how this is symptomatically expressed as ecological degradation of the land through extraction and pollution and the systematic marginalisation of peoples. He considers opportunities for reflection, remediation and reparation for this through designed reorientation toward the depth of the gift of Indigenous Australian sovereignty.

LOUISE CHIODO

Louise has a background in landscape architecture and cultural studies. Drawing on experiences and frameworks across both of these fields, Louise is interested in the ways in which cultural identities and particular power dynamics manifest through the design of the built environment, including the tensions and contradictions this creates, and how these are experienced. She is currently teaching into history, theory and design streams of landscape architecture, and completing her PhD in which she experiments with alternative modes of writing and representing space to uncover the often hidden histories of landscapes and their effects on our experiences of them today.

GABRIEL DÍAZ MONTEMAYOR

Gabriel Diaz Montemayor is an Assistant Professor of Landscape Architecture at The University of Texas, Austin. Being raised in northern Mexico, his teaching and research are focused on the social and environmental opportunities, found at multiple scales and in multiple actors, to reconcile urban with natural systems in the US-Mexico border and the American Southwest. Gabriel's academic studio assignments often engage with applied landscape architecture and urban design collaborative projects with public urban planning and design institutions in Mexican Cities. This has included works with cities such as Chihuahua, Hermosillo, Los Cabos, Nogales, Saltillo, and Ciudad Miguel Aleman, all in Mexico. Gabriel holds a Master of Landscape Architecture Degree from Auburn University and an Architect degree from the Autonomous University of Chihuahua. Gabriel has taught and lectured in various universities of the US, Mexico, Puerto Rico, Bolivia, Colombia, Panama, and Ecuador.

MELISSA GREEN

Hailing from New York, Melissa Green is a third year in the Harvard Graduate School of Design Master of Landscape Architecture program. Melissa's research lands between ecologically sensitive landscapes of resilience and actively critiquing the role of the designer in community engagement. She is particularly interested in incorporating vernacular tools and methods of communication into landscape architectural practice as a means of directly serving communities that have been historically denied access to landscape affordances. Melissa's experience as a horticulturist and community organiser, along with her undergraduate education in environmental studies and art at Skidmore College, has informed the integrative lens through which she understands the world.

ESTELLO RAGANIT

Estello Raganit is entering his third year as a Master of Landscape Architecture candidate at Harvard University's Graduate School of Design where his research interests lie in excavating and celebrating the landscape as a palimpsest of collective memories. His field analysis of public spaces appropriated by Beijing's underserved LGBTQ population has clarified a research agenda that imagines the coupling of landscape architectural practice with idiomatic forms of community-centered design. Growing up in Las Vegas, Nevada and having studied biology and English with a focus on race and ethnic studies at Vassar College, Estello positions the landscape as the medium through which we might broaden notions of sustainability to include the social, cultural, and political realms as a means of designing experientially rich and inclusive spaces.

FRONTIER MASSACRE RESEARCH TEAM

Dr Jennifer Debenham is a Senior Research Assistant in the Centre for the History of Violence at the University of Newcastle. Publications include The Australia Day Regatta (2014) with C Cheater. She recently submitted her monograph, Celluloid Lives: The Representation of Aboriginal People in Australian Documentary Film to ASP.

Dr Mark Brown Is Conjoint Fellow in the School of Humanities and Social Science at the University of Newcastle. He recently completed the cartography and online mapping for the Aboriginal Tasmania Story Project. His background is in spatial analysis and visualisation.

Prof Lyndall Ryan is Conjoint Professor in the Centre for the History of Violence at the University of Newcastle. Her recent books include ' Remembering the Myall Creek Massacre' (2018) with Jane Lydon, and 'Tasmanian Aborigines A History since 1803' (2012).

Dr William (Bill) Pascoe is a Digital Humanities specialist with the Centre For 21st Century Humanities and the Centre for Literary and Linguistic Computing at the University of Newcastle. His work is in eResearch focusing on web and software development projects with experience across finance, water engineering, science, health and humanities.

JEFA GREENAWAY

After working for a number of significant architectural practices Jefa established Greenaway Lowe in 2003. The practice changed name to Greenaway Architects in 2010 where Jefa has sought to build upon its reputation as an innovative and professional practice.

Educated at Melbourne and Latrobe universities, Jefa was the recipient of the AIA National Emerging Architect Prize - The Dulux Study Tour (2011), the Inaugural Stormtech Scholarship to the Glenn Murcutt International Master Class (2011) and participants in the British Council's Accelerate Leadership Intensive (2012).

He is currently a Lecturer in Construction and a Studio Leader at the Melbourne School of Design and the Robin Boyd Foundation's Residential Summer Design Studio Intensive.

MELANIE LI

Melanie Li is a Master of Architecture candidate at Carleton University in Ottawa, Canada. She will be starting her thesis year in Fall 2018, and will be looking to study gendered spaces and environments in urban theory and planning. She currently works at the Carleton Immersive Media Studio [CMIS} Lab, as part fo the digitally assisted storytelling stream. She is involved in designing and branding future public spaces that will serve to educate locals and tourists about the Canadian parliamentary system and on-going governmental projects.

NELSON BYRD WOLTZ

Nelson Byrd Woltz (NBW) Landscape Architects, with offices in Charlottesville, Virginia, New York City, and Melbourne, Australia, approaches each project with a commitment to research. This research provides our landscape architects with an understanding of the unique ecological and cultural stories of sites that will inform the design. Memorial landscapes, historic traditions adapted for the current world, and the rejuvenation of degraded and marginalised lands are examples of the contexts that ground NBW's work, which spans over four continents.

SOPHIA PEARCE

Sophia Pearce is a Barkandji woman from Gol Gol in south-west NSW. Sophia is currently completing a PhD in anthropology through La Trobe University situated in Mildura. Sophia's interest lies in preserving and protecting culture and heritage with particular reference to the management and repatriation of Barkandji cultural objects and places. In doing, Sophia's work supports the development and maintenance of cultural places and Indigenous ontology across disciplines, work which has been recognised with awards at state and national levels.

JOCK GILBERT

Jock is a registered landscape architect actively engaged with industry and community through an academic practice in the landscape architecture programs at RMIT University. Nationally, his work has received industry award recognition and he is regularly invited to contribute to professional discourse through critical commentary. His research and teaching are focussed around the convergence of concepts of place, Country and landscape through the western edge of the Murray-Darling Basin and the development of Indigenous-led frameworks through which to approach these concepts.

CHARLES MASSY

Charles Massy gained a Bachelor of Science at the Australian National University (ANU) in 1976 before going farming for thirty-five years and developing the prominent Merino sheep stud "Severn Park". Concern at ongoing land degradation and humanity's sustainability challenge led him to return to the ANU in 2009 to undertake a PhD in Human Ecology. Charles was awarded an Order of Australia Medal for his service as chair and director of a number of research organizations and statutory wool boards. He has also served on national and international review panels in sheep and wool research and development and genomics. Charles has authored several books on the Australian sheep industry, the most recent being the widely acclaimed Breaking the Sheep's Back , which was short-listed for the Prime Minister's Australian Literary Awards in Australian History in 2012.

ANNACATERINA PIRAS

Annacaterina Piras: LWCircus.org: Florence - Architect (1999), Cartographer (2004) and PhD in Landscape Architecture (2011). Annacaterin collaborates with different universities, foundations and cultural institutions, such as the Cornell University in Rome (2009), the Master in Landscape Architecture of Barcelona at ETSAB_UPC (2010), the RMIT University, School of Architecture and Design (Practice Research Symposium) from 2013 to present, the Bauhaus Dessau Foundation (2011) and the ENSP, Ecole nationale supérieure du Paysage, Versailles (2013-16), as well as the Universidad Marista, Merida (2016), the Chinese Universities of SCUA, SCUT, GAFA in Guangzhou and PKU, Beijing (2017), the UHM, University of Hawaii at Manoa (2017) and Turenscape Academy (from 2018). From 2009, She worked at the MMLU, Master in Mediterranean Landscape Urbanism, at the Alghero School of Architecture, University of Sassari, where she worked as Academic Coordinator for the second edition of the Masters (2014-2015). She is co-founder and has been scientific coordinator for the last six editions (2011-2016) of LandWorks-Sardinia International Program. She is Co-Founder and Scientific Coordinator of LWCircus, Italian - Mexican Operative Shared Program based on Social Practices.

STEPHANIE MURRAY

Stephanie is currently a Master of Archictecture candidate at the Azrieli School of Architecture in Ottawa, Canada. With a background in fine arts and a specialisation in ceramics, she has nurtured an appreciation of rich materiality and experiential based making that finds definition in the interaction between media and maker. She developed a sensitivity toward land engagement from time spent living in the Yukon and a childhood of urban agrarianism. She believes that design can shed light on real contemporary issues and inform narratives of change or caution. These positions have been solidified by visiting harsh environments with extreme physical and political landscapes, such as the Negev Desert and the Canadian Arctic.

OFFICE

Steve Mintern and Simon Robinson are directors of OFFICE. OFFICE is a multi-disciplinary not-for-profit whose remit is to use the tools of design, architecture and research for the public good. www.office.org.au